I IS FOR ILLUMINATI

AN A-Z GUIDE TO OUR PARANOID TIMES

CHRIS VOLA

ILLUSTRATED BY KENI THOMAS

MORROW
GIFT

An Imprint of WILLIAM MORROW

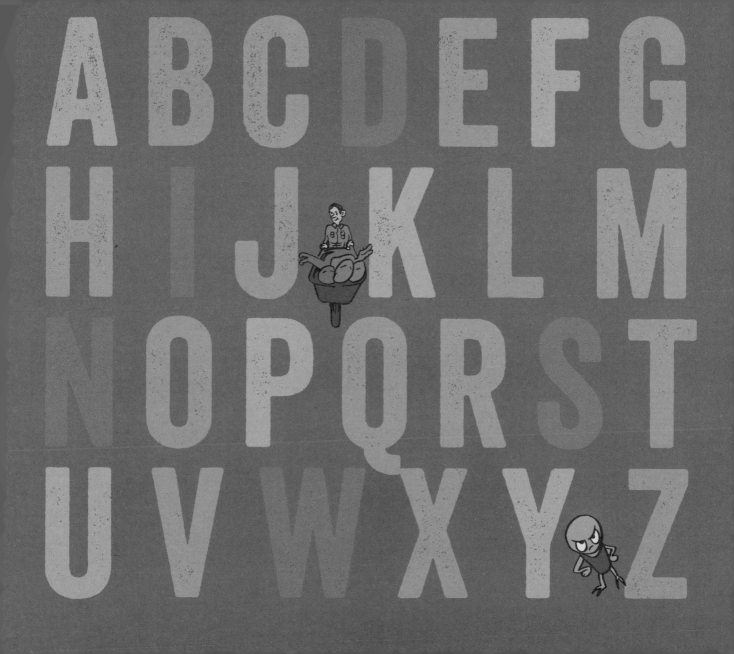

I IS FOR ILLUMINATI

AN A-Z GUIDE TO OUR PARANOID TIMES

A

IS FOR ALIENS

A is for Aliens, both ancient and new—

Grays, Blues, Reptilians, every conceivable hue.

You can stargaze all night, wait for saucers to appear

But isn't it more likely they're already here?

The Predator. ALF. Lieutenant Commander Worf. Your crazy cat lady neighbor who uses crystals to communicate with the little green ancestors she met on an acid trip at a Phish show twenty years ago. Most everyone's familiar with the fictional (we assume?) extraterrestrials that infiltrate our screens and lives, but what about the real thing? Is there a real thing?

Unidentified flying objects—and the creatures piloting them—have allegedly been entering Earth's atmosphere since long before people had cell phones to record those encounters. The oral traditions of ancient tribes like the Dogon in West Africa and the Hopi of the American Southwest speak of star beings descending from sky chariots to teach our primitive ancestors useful things like agriculture, medicine, and why a Capricorn should never date a Taurus. Numerous historical figures like Ramses II, Alexander the Great, and the Roman Emperor Constantine witnessed what they described as massive flaming shields or crosses streaking through the sky, which, in some cases, directly influenced the results of major battles. However, up until the twentieth century, most of these brushes with the unknown were chalked up to angels, witchcraft, or being dangerously overserved at the local mead spot.

The hysteria sparked by Orson Welles's 1938 radio narration of *The War of the Worlds* first thrust the idea of technologically advanced spacefarers into the mainstream cultural consciousness. Then, the supposed crash of a flying saucer in the desert outside of Roswell, New Mexico, in 1947 really got things heated up. The subsequent explosion of UFO sightings and claims of alien abductions stoked the public's imagination, provided a nice source of income for countless science-fiction writers, and, according to thousands of whistleblowers, sent the United States' military and defense industries into a tizzy.

From the alleged creation of clandestine 1940s ET-monitoring programs like Majestic 12 and Project Blue Book to President Dwight D. Eisenhower supposedly meeting with small, gray-skinned visitors at various air force bases in the 1950s; from claims of reverse-engineering faster-than-light-speed vehicles in places like Area 51 to recent revelations by former military employees about a decades-old space program called Solar Warden wherein humans have been secretly using that extraterrestrial technology to colonize the solar system and fight wars against evil Reptilian overlords from the Pleiades star cluster, the rumors of behind-the-scenes alien influencers have only gotten crazier as the years go by. Some researchers have even alleged that most so-called ETs aren't from other planets at all but are actually extradimensional, interdimensional, or trans-dimensional beings who have been traveling from their sub-universes to ours using worm-holes.

While anything alien- or UFO-related has historically been dismissed as the paranoid fodder of overly imaginative basement dwellers, dozens of highly credible sources have also come forward to offer some startling insights. Paul Hellyer, the former Canadian defense minister, has stated that there are approximately eighty extraterrestrial races visiting Earth at any given time, including nine-foot-tall "Nordics" with pale skin and blond hair, the commonly depicted short grays with their big heads and black slit eyes, and different types of bird- and lizard-headed creatures (similar to depictions of various ancient Egyptian deities). He claims that most of them are benevolent, and that their increased interest in us stems from their fear that our misuse of atomic energy will send the entire cosmos into a tailspin. Yikes.

Perhaps more shockingly, in the fall of 2019, the US Navy admitted that videos taken by pilots in 2004, which depicted a cigar-shaped craft performing seemingly impossible maneuvers—and were later featured by former Pentagon employee Luis Elizondo on the History Channel's *Unidentified: Inside America's UFO Investigation*—were indeed evidence of "unidentified aerial phenomena." It was the first time a government agency had ever explicitly confirmed the existence of UFOs, upending more than fifty years of absolute denial. It was also a victory for an unlikely coalition of truthers led by Elizondo, former Deputy Assistant Secretary of Defense for Intelligence Christopher Mellon, and former Blink-182 guitarist Tom DeLonge (yes, seriously).

To paraphrase TV's spookiest FBI agent, Fox Mulder, the truth is probably out there. But what if—in all likelihood—"there" is already "here"? What do our neighbors from the sky really want? Maybe, like Hellyer and others have speculated, they're here to help, surreptitiously saving us from nuclear disaster while slowly disseminating technology—yay, iPhones!—and disclosing their presence in a way that won't blow our collective, puny human brains.

Or maybe, like the grim reaper figures who supposedly heralded the arrival of the bubonic plague (and were also probably ETs), the UFOs shooting across the sky these days are markers of impending doom, and all the abductions are part of a massive experiment to create a hybrid human-alien race. Boo, forced evolution through genocide! Let's hope it's the former, because if any being capable of piloting a possibly interdimensional craft that goes from zero to fifteen million in less than a second wants to take us out, there's really nothing you, me, or Will Smith can do about it.

WHAT ELSE BEGINS WITH A?

Al Bielek

Alex Jones

Alternative Therapy Suppression

Anastasia Romanov

Antichrist

Antifa

Anti-Vaxxers

Anunnaki

Area 51

Art Bell

B

IS FOR
BERMUDA TRIANGLE

B is for Bermuda, the Triangle specifically.

Where things have a habit of disappearing terrifically.

Strange lights, deadly whirlpools, and forced teleportation

Might make you rethink your next cruise destination.

When considering Bermuda, you might think of pink sand beaches, pristine snorkeling opportunities, and pasty British legs unfortunately exposed by khaki short-shorts. But for most people, the stormy waters just to the south of the archipelago conjure a much more sinister vibe. Covering around five hundred thousand square miles of the Atlantic Ocean and Caribbean Sea, the Bermuda Triangle (also known as the Devil's Triangle) is best known for the disturbing number of ships and aircraft that have vanished or been found mysteriously abandoned while traversing the area. Though it was first brought to light in a 1950 *Miami Herald* article, the phenomenon had been occurring for years, including the 1919 disappearance of the US Navy cargo ship USS *Cyclops* and its 306-person crew, representing the largest single noncombat loss of life in American military history.

There have been hundreds of similar accidents. An entire fleet of torpedo bomber planes seemingly evaporated into the clouds in 1945.

A collision between two military aircraft somehow leaving two separate debris fields 160 miles apart from each other. A seaplane pilot named Bruce Gernon flying into some fog and suddenly finding himself 100 miles off course in the blink of an astonished eye. Despite this, mainstream scientists and various busybodies (including more than a few government-contracted "aeronautics experts") have always given predictably boring explanations for the disappearances and accidents: magnetic anomalies, bad weather, rogue waves, or that meddlesome Gulf Stream are some of their favorite go-tos.

However, thousands of pilots and other eyewitnesses tell a different story, describing an outrageous assortment of inexplicable happenings. Sudden jumps in time, teleportation-inducing electronic fog, underwater vortexes, mesmerizing lights flickering under the waves and across the sky, Nazi ghost ships, and Google Earth images of what appear to be submerged spacecraft, are all par for this odd course.

Taking that weirdness to the next level, the early twentieth-century psychic Edgar Cayce decreed (from a vision) that the lost city of Atlantis had sunk near the Bahamas thousands of years earlier. When what appeared to be megalithic structures were discovered off the coast of Bimini Island, several of his followers claimed that they had powered the Atlantean civilization. Their theory was that these giant crystals must still be radiating massive amounts of energy that had to be the main source of aircraft and ship malfunctions in the area. Though buzzkill archaeologists immediately dismissed the structures as natural formations, a group of oceanic surveyors added more fuel to that fire in 2000 when they discovered what appeared to be pyramid-like structures sunk deep below the waters off Cuba. Their sonar imagery was so compelling that, in 2004, the National Geographic Society agreed to finance a second expedition and feature any findings in its magazine . . . only to sketchily pull out at the last minute, leaving any potentially history-altering answers safely buried deep beneath the waves. Hmm.

Despite the Triangle's deadly reputation, casualties are relatively rare in what is one of the most highly trafficked shipping lanes in the world. But if you do find yourself on a cruise ship in the area, it might be best to take advantage of the all-you-can-eat buffet in case the bloodthirsty, all-it-can-eat ocean decides it's ready for another meal.

WHAT ELSE BEGINS WITH B?

Bank for International Settlements
Benghazi
Big Pharma
Bilderberg Group
Bob Lazar
Bohemian Grove
Breitbart

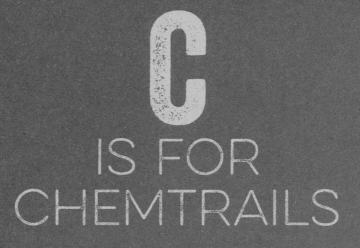

C
IS FOR
CHEMTRAILS

C is for Chemtrails that fill the airways with vapors,

"Harmless plane condensation," say the leading newspapers.

But those in the know see a more sinister sky—

Mind control, biological warfare, radiation, oh my!

Ever notice how aircraft and rockets leave behind vapor trails that linger for a few minutes after they fly over? Yeah? Ever have any thoughts about them longer than, "Ah, look at the pretty cloud streak things!"? Probably not. But those harmless-looking spurts of condensation, or contrails, have begun to scare the begeezus out of a growing number of concerned citizens who believe that some of them contain much more than just frozen water and a bit of engine exhaust.

Popularized by radio host Art Bell and several internet forum jockeys in the 1990s, the idea is that shady government types (who else?) have been secretly lacing aircraft engines with dangerous biological agents in order to create "chemtrails" that shower these invisible substances onto an unsuspecting populace. The reason? That depends on who you ask. Most believers think it has to do with stopping overpopulation, that the chemicals are supposed to kill off the old and weak and sterilize the rest of us. Other popular motives include mind control, DNA regulation, and weather manipulation (see page 33).

As far as hard evidence goes, there isn't much, but theorists claim that chemtrails appear thicker and last longer than normal contrails, and that this type of emission has only been seen in recent years (despite World War II–era photographs showing similar trails). They also refer to the *Space Preservation Act of 2001*, a bill introduced by US congressman Dennis Kucinich that explicitly listed chemtrails as a space-based weapon; the bill was quickly shot down by the Department of Defense.

Scientists and aircraft manufacturers point out that the reason some contrails stay in the sky longer than others has everything to do with weather conditions and nothing to do with their composition. Others use logic, asking why any nation wishing to sustain itself would want to knowingly poison and sterilize its people. None of that does anything to deter the hardcore chemtrail crowd, who view all the energy that's been spent debunking the theory over the past two decades—including multiple joint statements by organizations like the Environmental Protection Agency, the Federal Aviation Administration, and the National Oceanic and Atmospheric Administration, numerous speeches by politicians from both major parties, and constant ridicule from the mainstream media—as absolute proof that it's really happening.

Even if there's nothing nefarious going on, as common sense suggests, studies by NASA have shown that when it comes to the environment, contrails definitely aren't benign. They frequently expand and morph into cirrus clouds, which, in the short term, block sunlight and lower local temperatures. Paradoxically, they also tend to trap heat, leading to a rise in overall global temperature that's only going to get worse as the air traffic industry continues to expand. Which is certainly a bummer and something to be mindful of when deciding between a multiflight Europe trip or an environmentally friendly staycation, but it's nice to know we aren't being singled out for population control. Probably.

WHAT ELSE BEGINS WITH C?

CERN (European Organization
for Nuclear Research)
CIA
Cold Fusion
Committee of 300
Corey Goode
Council on Foreign Relations
Crack
Cults
Cultural Marxism

IS FOR DENVER INTERNATIONAL AIRPORT

D is for Denver, I mean the airport outside it,

Where weird stuff's happening, and they don't try to hide it.

Satanic murals, Masonic symbols, tunnels under the street,

A nifty post-apocalyptic summer camp for the global elite!

Ask a bunch of different people to describe the amenities in an ideal airport and you'll get a lot of similar responses: a convenient location, short walking distances between concourses, good food options, free Wi-Fi access, and a secret underground bunker system big enough to shelter several hundred industrial and political elites in the event of a moderate to apocalyptic global catastrophe. Okay, probably not that last one. But that's just one of several alleged features that make Denver International Airport one of the most interesting—and creepiest—structures in the world for the conspiratorially minded.

Completed in February 1995 (sixteen months late and $2 billion over budget) at the unheard of cost of $4.8 billion, Denver International is more than twice the size of Manhattan and seven times larger than Stapleton International, the more easily accessible airport that it replaced. If its inexplicably massive size isn't enough to pique your interest, then you're in luck, because DIA's designers made sure to stuff every corner of the place with bizarre art, odd structures, and suggestive symbolism. Swastika-shaped runways, giant murals featuring the Egyptian death god Anubis, children huddled around burning buildings and knives, pseudo-Nazi soldiers, and haunting visions of biological warfare, and a thirty-two-foot-tall, nine-thousand-pound mustang statue with terrifying red eyes that fell over during its construction and fatally crushed the artist who created it. You know, just the kind of soothing ambiance that really gets rid of the preflight jitters!

The capstone placed in the airport to commemorate DIA's dedication features a large Masonic square and compasses symbol, as well as a list of the airport's primary benefactors, including something called the "New World Airport Commission." Strangely, this organization doesn't actually exist. This is a reference to the New World Order, a clandestine cabal linked to Freemasonry and allegedly comprised of some seriously powerful people (including, perhaps, the Antichrist) who have been secretly plotting for centuries to replace all sovereign nation-states with an authoritarian world government. One way they supposedly plan to accomplish this is by orchestrating a series of worldwide catastrophes, which directly ties in to what might be lurking below Denver International—and why it was so expensive to build.

Several DIA construction workers have described a massive tunnel system and five large subterranean buildings that would make an ideal place to run a global shadow government, a claim, oddly enough, that's backed by public figures like former governor-wrestler Jesse Ventura. Other rumors include an underground network of cities populated by aliens, technologically advanced fallout shelters for the überwealthy, and a ready-made FEMA concentration camp for any nonelite unlucky enough to survive the various apocalypses. Airport officials have been quick to dismiss any such theories, stating that the tunnels are simply part of a boring old underground rail system. Sure, sure.

Looking for some of the most blatant evidence of a dark presence that's pulling the strings behind the scenes, gleefully tearing apart our society root and stem? Just hop on the next flight to Colorado and wander through Earth's creepiest airport. But maybe steer clear of the giant evil horse while you're there.

WHAT ELSE BEGINS WITH D?

David Icke

Deep State

Deepwater Horizon

Deep Web

Dogon Tribe

Donald Trump

Dwight Eisenhower

E
IS FOR
EARTH

E is for Earth, a place we all know,

But what about what's above it, inside it, and below?

Is it flat? Is it hollow? Is the globe obsolete?

Do you trust the laws of physics or your favorite athlete?

Before their first morning of school, when they walk into their classroom and see a globe sitting on their teacher's desk, the average child already takes for granted that Earth is a sphere. Which is nothing new. Since the time of Aristotle in the fourth century BCE, the overwhelming majority of philosophers, scientists, and members of the learned classes have generally agreed on the planet's roundness, with many of them devising increasingly accurate methods of measuring Earth's circumference.

However, no amount of science (and common sense) has been enough to sway members of the Flat Earth movement, a centuries-old fringe group whose numbers have swelled recently thanks in part to YouTube and the support of noted intellectual luminaries like NBA player Kyrie Irving, rapper B.o.B., and bubbly 2000s internet persona Tila Tequila. Typically, flat-earthers believe that, because they can't see the curvature of the earth with their own eyes, the planet must be disc-shaped, with the North Pole at its center, and the sun and moon (which are much smaller than scientists suggest) revolving around it in a geocentric orbit. According to them, Earth is completely surrounded by Antarctica, which is actually a giant wall of ice. The reason that no one's ever proven the existence of said wall is because it's apparently being guarded by the US military, who, along with NASA and just about every other government in the world, are conspiring to hide the planet's true shape from the public.

In fact, flat-earthers claim that most space travel has been faked—including the moon landings (see page 53)—and that the hundreds of thousands of photographs taken of the Earth from space have all been doctored. But why the secrecy? Flat-earthers don't really have an answer to that question, or how the world's leaders could possibly perpetuate a global hoax that would require millions of government employees to keep their mouths shut and cost billions of dollars annually. Still, mountains of evidence to the contrary (most recently a successful demonstration of Earth's curvature recorded by

National Geographic at the Salton Sea in June 2018) have done little to deter the thousands of flat-earthers across the, ahem, globe. If anything, you have to admire their persistence.

What's going on inside Earth is a bit more of a gray area. From the most ancient times, nearly every culture has been fascinated by the idea of an underworld lurking beneath our feet. It's been imagined as everything from a place of darkness and dead souls, like the Hades of Greek mythology; to a technologically advanced kingdom populated by advanced beings, like the Buddhist Agartha; to a wacky prehistoric wilderness filled with dinosaurs and giant mushrooms, as in Jules Verne's novel *Journey to the Center of the Earth* and the (very terrible) film version starring Brendan Fraser. And while the current consensus is that the subterranean Earth is composed solely of dense crusts, liquid magma, and a scalding-hot nickel and iron core, so far humans have only drilled a measly eight miles inward. Meaning, we don't know for sure.

Scientific speculation about the possibility of a Hollow Earth has been occurring at least since the time of Edmond Halley (yes, the Halley's comet guy), who theorized that large underground concentric voids were responsible for magnetic anomalies and faulty compass readings. Other mathematicians and astronomers soon began to push the idea of a tiny second sun suspended at the Earth's center, one capable of sustaining life in the planet's underbelly, a realm that could only be entered through massive holes at the North and South Poles. Hollow-earthers have been proposing journeys to these access points since at least 1822, when activist John Cleves Symmes Jr. nearly convinced Congress to fund a polar expedition. In the twentieth century, a few men claimed to have seen the inner Earth, including German U-boat sailor Karl Unger and Rear Admiral Richard E. Byrd, a highly respected US naval officer who in 1947 allegedly wrote a secret diary entry about flying over lush tropical forests and a herd of woolly mammoths in the area where the North Pole should have been.

Aliens, highly evolved humanoids capable of living for thousands of years, fifteen-foot giants, and escaped Nazis have all been suggested as residents of the Hollow Earth, but good luck trying to get close to them. Planes are forbidden from flying over either pole due to possible "navigation issues" (mm-hmm) and proposed seagoing voyages like 2014's privately funded North Pole Inner Earth Expedition (NPIEE)—which would have used a nuclear-powered Russian icebreaker to force its way through the Arctic—have been derailed by catastrophic setbacks such as crew members dying from mysterious cancers or in unexplained plane crashes. Several of NPIEE's investors pulled out at the last moment because, according to some expedition leaders, they were pressured by an international banking conspiracy. Meaning, if you're getting the itch to do some polar/inner Earth exploration of your own, maybe watch Brendan Fraser avoid getting eaten by carnivorous plants until the urge leaves you.

WHAT ELSE BEGINS WITH E?

Ebola Epidemic
Edgar Cayce
Electric Car Suppression
Electronic Surveillance
Elvis Presley

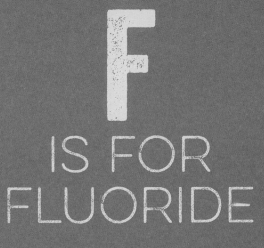

IS FOR
FLUORIDE

F is for the Fluoride in the water you drink,

It helps prevent cavities, so what's the big stink?

How about a bum thyroid, brain damage, and forced sterilization—

Good luck fighting the Man with no pineal motivation!

How does the old saying go? A glass of tap water a day keeps the dentist away?

Maybe not. But that was—officially—why the US Public Health Service began to encourage communities to lace their drinking water with small amounts of the tooth-strengthening chemical fluoride in the 1940s, a practice that, for the most part, continues to expand globally to this day. At face value, it does seem like a smart idea, considering that most children in industrialized countries suffer some level of tooth decay. Studies have shown that cavity rates are significantly lower in areas that practice fluoridation, saving billions of dollars in health care costs and making it much easier to achieve that pearly-white, Instagrammable smile.

Despite the best available scientific evidence consistently indicating that water fluoridation is totally safe—and the backing of more than one hundred domestic and international health organizations—some scientists argue that the practice's benefits have been overstated, that it actually might cause long-term bone weakening, and is pretty much obsolete at this point due to the widespread, regular use of fluoride toothpaste. Other political groups, religious factions, and alternative medical practitioners question the ethics of not allowing individuals to choose what kind of water they can access.

But that's nothing compared to the shade that OG fluoride haters have thrown for the past seventy years. Far-right activists in the 1940s and 1950s alleged that fluoridation was part of a plot by President Truman to socialize medicine in order to eventually impose a communist regime on the American people, a fear that was revived by many viewers of Stanley Kubrick's similarly themed 1964 film *Dr. Strangelove*. In the eighties, researcher Ian E. Stephens published a booklet in which he claimed that "repeated doses of infinitesimal amounts of fluoride will in time reduce an individual's power to resist domination by slowly poisoning and narcotizing a certain area of the brain and will thus make him submissive to the will of those who wish to govern him," specifically referring to the pineal gland, the part of the brain responsible for producing melatonin and protecting the body from cell damage caused by free radicals.

Contemporary antifluoride crusaders also frequently mention Stephens's disputed claim that the German and Soviet governments in World War II added sodium fluoride to their military prisoners' water to make them "stupid and docile." While the US government has firmly denied all of the alleged conspiracies, it's interesting to note that in 2006, the National Research Council recommended lowering the maximum amount of fluoride in US drinking water, officially citing for the first time the potential hazards of extreme fluoridation.

Even with all of the controversies, it looks like fluoride will be an inescapable part of the water most of us drink for the foreseeable future. But hey, on the off chance that your mind is slowly being eroded to make you a docile slave to the evil government and industrial overlords, at least your teeth will look great in that next profile pic!

WHAT ELSE BEGINS WITH F?
False Flags
FBI
FDA
Federal Reserve
Flying Saucers
Free Energy Suppression
Freemasonry

G
IS FOR
GIANTS

G is for Giants, whose bones were found across nations,

Until the Scientific Establishment sent men to halt excavations.

"Darwin was right!" they hollered. "His theory needs no replacement!"

And that's why those bones are locked in somebody's basement.

"Fifty Skeletons Unearthed—Remains of Giant Aborigines Discovered." "Giant Indian Bones: Discovery of an Extraordinary Skeleton Near Fond Du Lac." "Atlantis in the Colorado River Desert." "The Horned Skull of Sayre, Pennsylvania." "New Mexico Discovery: 12-Foot Giant Found."

Though the above quotes might read like plot points from a creepy science-fiction or historical fantasy novel, they're all actual headlines that appeared in legitimate newspapers across the United States in the nineteenth and early twentieth centuries. The last one was from the February 11, 1902, edition of a plucky little rag called the *New York Times* (maybe you've heard of it). And those are just a fraction of the hundreds of articles, diaries, and other firsthand writings from that time period from people who stumbled upon the remains of ancient, impossibly massive humans that would have stood between seven and twelve feet tall, many with extremely strange physical characteristics like double rows of teeth, horn-like spurs protruding from their skulls, and bright red hair. Many of these accounts have been compiled by author Richard J. Dewhurst in *The Ancient Giants Who Ruled America,* alongside published descriptions of spectacular stone and earthen tombs, bodies wrapped in precious gems, copper weapons of an almost impossible purity, and the remains of large-scale mining operations, cities, fortifications, and monument complexes apparently stretching back tens of thousands of years—the last remnants of a vast, forgotten civilization.

But if these finds were supposedly so commonplace, how have they been almost completely erased from our cultural consciousness? Especially given humanity's longtime fascination with giants, from Homer's cyclops to the Nephilim and Goliath of the Bible? According to Dewhurst, one need look no further than a racist buzzkill named John Wesley Powell, who headed the Smithsonian Institution's Bureau of Ethnography from 1879 to 1902. A staunch Darwinist, Powell declared any purported giant bones to be a hoax. According to his view of evolution, humans had been growing bigger, smarter, and stronger in a linear fashion, and implied that he and his (white) brethren represented the apex of the species, a concept that anyone who believes that birds descended from dinosaurs would find laughable. Unfortunately, many Americans shared his opinion and considered the Smithsonian an absolute archaeological authority (see page 87). They ridiculed the idea that a race as "primitive" as the Native Americans could descend from physically superior beings intelligent enough to master coppersmithing, written languages, and the ability to cultivate an advanced society. It's no surprise that the majority of the finds in Dewhurst's book were allegedly handed off to Smithsonian agents, their contents swiftly excavated, and never seen again.

Mainstream archaeology's stance on America's past has wavered little in the last century or so, but cracks in the armor are beginning to show. Recent digs have unearthed evidence showing that the story of the continent is far older and more complex than anyone could have imagined. Examples include a site in South Carolina that predates the area's accepted settlement date by 30,000 years and a human-worked mammoth bone found under a highway in San Diego that's reportedly been carbon-dated to 150,000 years ago. Perhaps, if we dig deeper and longer, we may find evidence of our over-sized ancestors that no government busybody will be able to deny.

Or, if you're feeling impatient, you could always knock on the Smithsonian's front door and ask about giant bones. But good luck with that.

WHAT ELSE BEGINS WITH G?

Gary McKinnon
George Soros
Getty Family
Global Government
Global Warming
GMOs
Graham Hancock
Grand Canyon
Great Replacement

IS FOR
HAARP

H is for HAARP, an acronym that's pretty

Except this research program's motives are most likely real shitty.

Controlling the weather to make crops grow faster?

Sounds more like a scapegoat for engineering natural disasters . . .

According to the University of Alaska Fairbanks, its High-frequency Active Auroral Research Program, or HAARP, is "a scientific endeavor aimed at studying the properties and behavior of the ionosphere," one that allows scientists "to better understand processes that occur continuously under the natural stimulation of the sun." A little wordy, a little nerdy, but it seems fairly innocuous, yes? Where's the harm in studying the short-term atmospheric changes that are affected by Earth and the sun? Wouldn't it be helpful to be better at forecasting and preparing for things like solar flares, magnetic storms, and other space-related phenomena? Improving the performance of navigation and communications systems? Sounds great, right?

Well, sure. But since HAARP's establishment by the US Navy and Air Force in 1993, many have argued that what's going on at the secretive program's sub-Arctic facility is far different from what it reveals to the public—and much more terrifying. Like, destroy-the-planet terrifying. Dozens of rogue scientists and political insiders believe that HAARP is nothing less than a fully operational military weapon that, like chemtrails, controls the weather to wreak havoc on anything or anyone it chooses to target. Canadian economist Michel Chossudovsky suggests that HAARP could easily trigger all manner of natural disasters like floods, hurricanes, droughts, and earthquakes. Which is definitely disconcerting, but nowhere near as extreme as some of the capabilities that others have claimed. We're talking giant lenses that can turn the atmosphere into a ball of fire and shower the Earth in mind-controlling rays, electron blasters that can neutralize or disable satellites and flip the planet's magnetic poles, even a diabolical machine that manipulates and traps peoples' souls.

While modern life has often been described as "soul-sucking," there's thankfully no hard evidence of any existing device that could actually achieve this. Government-sanctioned weather modification, on the other hand, is known to have been happening for decades. Starting in the 1940s, drought-prone countries have been "seeding" clouds with substances like silver iodide to alter precipitation, with little regard for potential flood damage and chemical side effects. Cloud seeding was even weaponized in the 1970s during the highly classified Operation Popeye, when the US military was able to prolong the East Asian monsoon season in support of its war efforts. It's not a stretch to assume that someone has continued to develop this technology in private, and the thousands of images and videos of massive, geometrically perfect clouds—some of them making hissing or humming sounds—that have exploded across the internet in the 2010s seem to confirm that something weird is indeed happening over our heads.

When it comes to transparency, the folks at HAARP aren't doing themselves any favors. Despite officially cutting ties with the military, the program is still known as one of the most enigmatic federally funded research facilities in the country, keeping its doors closed to just about anybody who tries to gain access to its secrets, including a documentary crew led by (who else) Jesse Ventura. But if you're really curious about the weirdo eggheads who spend their lives holed up in a creepy lab in the middle of the frozen tundra (i.e., the kind of people who probably want nothing more than to unleash a weather apocalypse on the guys who tormented them during gym class dodgeball), HAARP now hosts an annual open house each August for anyone who wants to tour its complex. Umm, no thanks. I think I'll take a rain check.

WHAT ELSE BEGINS WITH H?

Haiti Earthquake

Henry Kissinger

Hoaxes

Holocaust Revisionism

Hoover Dam

Hurricane Katrina

I

IS FOR
ILLUMINATI

I is for Illuminati, a group that wields secret knowledge,

Not the kind used for good, or what you might learn in college.

It's the kind that enslaves, takes away the freedoms you had.

Don't like the New World Order, buddy?

Well that's just too damn bad.

Everybody wants to rule the world.

No phrase encapsulates humanity's desire for power better than the title of new wave band Tears for Fears's 1985 hit single. But who, if anyone, does control the planet? Politicians? Military leaders? Bankers? Rap moguls? Tech giants? Mickey Mouse? A secretive cabal containing elements from all of the above?

In a discussion about who actually pulls the strings, those of the self-described "woke" variety will almost always point to the Illuminati, a name that has been given to several confirmed or alleged groups over the past few centuries. The first of these, the Bavarian Illuminati, were an offshoot of the Freemasons who were active in—you guessed it—Bavaria starting in the 1770s. This society of antigovernment and antireligious intellectuals was outlawed by Duke Charles Theodore and the Catholic Church in 1790, but supposedly continued operating on the down-low, even influencing the outcomes of the French Revolution and the Battle of Waterloo.

Today, the term "Illuminati" refers to purported organizations claimed by researchers to have descended from the Bavarians, but whose grip on our society is far stronger—and far more sinister—than that of their predecessors. Implicated in nearly every modern conspiracy theory, these are the real versions of the shadowy villains that appear in countless books, movies, TV shows, and video games; the vicious masterminds working behind the scenes to shape the world in their own, twisted image; the true architects of the coming authoritarian New World Order. Spooky, huh? More than happy to eliminate anyone who won't cooperate with their agenda (which allegedly includes mind control through all forms of media, human trafficking, and child sacrifice) or threatens to reveal it, they're allegedly responsible for taking out everyone from Tupac, Princess Diana, and Michael Jackson to Jeffrey Epstein and John F. Kennedy, who once spoke out against a "monolithic and ruthless conspiracy that relies on covert means for expanding its influence." Maybe JFK should have fired his speechwriter after that one.

So how can you tell who's an Illuminati affiliate? The short answer, according to theorists, is anyone in any position of power. That includes entire rosters of elite economic and foreign policy think tanks like the Bilderberg Group and the Council on Foreign Relations (whose members include people like Henry Kissinger and Warren Buffet), nearly every major political figure, and pop-culture icons like Madonna, Kanye West, Jay-Z, Beyoncé, Lady Gaga, LeBron James, and most, if not all, of the Kardashians/Jenners.

But where's the proof? Researchers point to the Illuminati's supposed love of Satanic and occult imagery (because of course they're Satanists and occultists), and its prevalence in society. Examples include the Eye of Horus, which figures prominently on the back of the American one-dollar bill; numerous hand gestures that appear in countless celebrity photographs (the fingertip triangle of power popularized by the aforementioned Jay-Z; the "OK" symbol around a person's eye that's thought to represent "666"; or the Mark of the Beast, the sign of the horns, duh); and the accounts of Hollywood insiders like Angelina Jolie, who was caught on tape in 1999 discussing bloody, S and M–style Illu-minati initiation rituals. A recent interview with Jolie's ex-husband Brad Pitt, in which the actor claimed that the movie industry was run by elite pedophiles, was quickly dismissed as a hoax by—you guessed it—the mainstream media.

Skeptics argue that there's really no hard evidence to support a conspiracy of this magnitude, that a group as secretive as the Illuminati would never allow itself to become so mainstream (or grant Kim Kardashian a membership). But, unlike the Flat Earth theory, no one's ever been able to prove that the Illuminati *doesn't* exist. And until somebody does, those dastardly world-mongers will always be lurking in the back of the cultural consciousness. If they do decide to come for you, just flash a triangle symbol and tell them you loved Jay-Z's last album.

WHAT ELSE BEGINS WITH I?

Infowars
International Order of St. Hubertus
Iran-Contra
ISIS

J

IS FOR
J. EDGAR HOOVER

J is for J. Edgar Hoover, the FBI's first director,

No one's ever swung a bigger stick in the intelligence sector,

A master of blackmail, coercion, and the state-sanctioned lie,

You'd have to be fearless (or stupid) to mess with this guy.

Shortly after John Edgar Hoover's death in 1972, President Richard Nixon eulogized the Washington, DC, native who, for the previous forty-eight years, had garnered unprecedented notoriety (as well as plenty of fear) as director of the FBI, describing him as "one of the giants . . . a national symbol of courage, patriotism, and granite-like honesty and integrity." Sure, most people probably wouldn't consider Nixon a particularly great judge of character. Even so, it's hard to downplay Hoover's role in shaping American law enforcement culture. From taking down notorious 1930s bank robbers like Machine Gun Kelly and apprehending Nazi agents on American soil during World War II, to decoding Soviet spy communications and infiltrating domestic political organizations, J. Edgar redefined what a crime fighter could do, and turned the FBI into a technically savvy juggernaut of justice whose agents were almost universally considered heroes.

But with great power comes great paranoia, and no one was more suspicious of his fellow citizens than the director. In order to maintain power and, ostensibly, the existing social and political order, Hoover closely monitored anyone he considered a threat (Communists, civil rights activists, progressive politicians, "deviant" celebrities, Charlie Chaplin, John Lennon, your mom, and pretty much everyone else) and employed any shady tactic he could get away with—illegal wiretaps, blackmail, psychological warfare, intimidation, violence, disseminating false documents, feeding the media fake news, wrongful imprisonment—to subdue them. He also apparently kept incriminating files on every president he served under to ensure he'd never be fired. As nosy as he was when it came to digging up his enemies' personal deets, he aggressively fought to keep his own life private, even if it meant going against the ethical code he claimed to live by. Shockingly, he denied the existence of the entire American Mafia in the 1950s, supposedly to cover up his own horse-betting addiction and because certain gangsters had compromising photographic evidence of a tryst between Hoover and his long-time boy toy Clyde Tolson.

The most infamous years of Hoover's career came in the 1960s, due to the FBI's alleged involvement in the assassinations of Martin Luther King Jr., John F. Kennedy, and Robert F. Kennedy. While no smoking-gun evidence of the purported conspiracies has yet emerged, Hoover made no secret of his dislike of all three men, especially King, to whom he sent a letter suggesting that the revered civil rights icon should commit suicide. Two days after JFK's death, Hoover ordered his underlings to consider the matter closed, which seems super odd since the person who just died was the leader of the free world and his own boss. In 1979, the House of Representatives issued a report criticizing Hoover for not investigating the assassinations further and chastising the FBI for allowing their leader to rule unchecked for nearly half a century. But the fact that the hearings didn't take place until seven years after Hoover died made one thing abundantly clear: while he was alive, you did not mess with the director.

It's easy to imagine how enamored Hoover would be of our current 24/7 surveillance culture, a world of drones and CCTV where those with badges or political clout scare us average Joes into being content to live by one of J. Edgar's most popular maxims: "Why should you care if you have nothing to hide?" At this point it's probably best just to smile and wave into your phone's webcam and (silently!) blame J. Edgar for whoever's on the other side analyzing the kitten memes you just sent to your possibly subversive group chat.

WHAT ELSE BEGINS WITH J?

Jade Helm 15
Jeffrey Epstein
Jesse Ventura
Jimmy Hoffa
John Birch Society
Jonestown

K

IS FOR KENNEDY

K is for Kennedy, a family with a history that's tragic,

But when you get power, you make enemies,

it doesn't happen by magic.

Jack and Bobby rubbed folks the wrong way, that much history shows,

But who did them in? The CIA or the Cubans?

Just a couple average Joes.

FRIDAY, NOVEMBER 22, 1963

A date that shocked the world, rattled the American political establishment, and spawned countless conspiracies and pop-culture references. The assassination of President John F. Kennedy is, without a doubt, one of the twentieth century's defining moments. What's less certain are the events leading up to that tragic afternoon in Dallas.

Sure, there's the Warren Commission's official explanation—promoted by super trustworthy people like our good friend Director Hoover—that a former US Marine and disgruntled Marxist named Lee Harvey Oswald acted alone, shooting the president from his perch in the Texas School Book Depository. But after Oswald's immediate and vehement denial of the crime, and his too convenient murder at the hands of nightclub owner and all-around shady character Jack Ruby a couple of days later, many people began to doubt that narrative. And most still do. According to various polls taken in the 2010s, only around 30 percent

of Americans side with the government's story, choosing instead to believe that Oswald was part of a much larger conspiracy. Unconfirmed allegations of multiple gunmen, multiple bullets, eyewitness tampering, and the destruction of medical and photographic evidence have run rampant for almost six decades. More than two hundred people have been accused of bearing some responsibility for the killing at one time or another.

Maybe it was the Mafia. As the scion of a well-connected family that made its fortune partially through illegal activities like bootlegging, who'd also recently signed anti-racketeering legislation, JFK certainly would have had more than a few underworld enemies. Or maybe, as a Communist sympathizer, Oswald was working with the Cubans or the KGB, who clearly weren't fans of JFK after, you know, that whole Bay of Pigs thing. Then there's the CIA, who, according to researchers, had any number of alleged reasons for wanting to do the deed, from its preference for the apparently more malleable and slightly more conservative Lyndon Johnson, to stopping JFK from ordering the organization to disclose all of the information it had on aliens and UFOs to the public. Just a guess, but forcing the nation's top spies to reveal stuff about their spying probably isn't the smartest career move, even for the world's most powerful man.

The CIA has also been implicated by researchers in the 1968 killing of JFK's brother, US senator Robert F. Kennedy, another progressive rabble-rouser who, at a presidential campaign rally, took a bullet from Sirhan Sirhan, a Palestinian immigrant who many believe was also a possible brainwashed asset (also known as a "Manchurian candidate") or a patsy for someone else in the crowd.

Both shootings have been deemed open-and-shut cases by several subsequent (government-funded) investigations and by the FBI. But for those still calling BS, some thirty thousand documents related to the Kennedy incidents were released to the public by the National Archives in 2017 and 2018, including an eyebrow-raising Hoover memo. With another batch of documents slated to be released in October 2021, maybe theorists will finally get some of the peace of mind they've been searching for.

Since the 1960s, peace has generally been in short supply for the Kennedy family, whose members have been beset by numerous calamities, including deadly car accidents, suicides, drug overdoses, aggressive cancers, and plane crashes—like the one that killed JFK's only son, John F. Kennedy Jr. US senator Ted Kennedy, brother of JFK and RFK (as well as a multicrash survivor and cancer victim), was known to lament his family's unusually bad luck. Maybe the "Kennedy Curse"—and not some wild international conspiracy—had already doomed Jack and Bobby from the start.

WHAT ELSE BEGINS WITH K?

KGB

Knights Templar

Ku Klux Klan

Kurt Cobain

IS FOR
LIZARD PEOPLE

L is for the Lizard People who've infiltrated our ranks,

From politicians to CEOs, from Hollywood to the banks.

You can stay off the grid all you like, but there's really no vacation,

From shapeshifting humanoid gators with

thoughts of world domination.

Do you have hazel, blue, or green eyes that others would describe as "piercing"? Do they often seem to change colors? Is your hair red or reddish? Do you feel a deep connection to outer space and a sense of not belonging to the human race? Do you have any unexplained scars or psychic abilities? Are you descended from royalty? If you answered "yes" to any of these questions, you might be a lizard person.

Championed by former sports broadcaster and professional conspiracy guru David Icke, the idea goes like this: millennia ago, reptilian-looking aliens from the constellations Draco, Sirius, and Orion landed on Earth and began manipulating and combining human DNA with their own, eventually creating a distinct subspecies with extraordinary abilities and bloodlines that exist to this day. Icke claims that evidence of biological meddling can be found in the Bible's Old Testament, especially in the story of the Garden of Eden, where the serpent's "tempting" of Adam and Eve was actually an advanced form of genetic engineering.

But what was the point? What did the reptilians want for our species? And what's the endgame? According to a growing number of theorists, the answer's obvious: to rule over the planet and turn the rest of humanity into mindless slaves through a fear-based, transnational control system. Duh! Apparently every ruling family that's existed on Earth since the dawn of civilization—from the Sumerian kings to the British monarchy and the American elite—has the same hybrid blood and has been in on this Illuminati-esque plot, one that's still going strong thanks to the current generation of lizard bankers, royals, presidents, and prime ministers who extensively manipulate the media and politics; control most of the planet's food, water, and air supply; and provide easy access to brain-numbing pharmaceuticals, booze, and nicotine.

That all might sound positively bonkers, but it's hard to ignore the connection between serpent worship and royalty in dozens of far-flung ancient cultures, including the Babylonians, Vikings, Zulu, Native Americans, Hindus, Greeks, and Aboriginal Australians. Statues and effigies of reptile-like gods have been found on every continent, and several dynasties, such as the ancient Chinese emperors and Egyptian pharaohs, defended their right to rule explicitly based on their supposed serpentine heritage. Reddish hair and elongated skulls are surprisingly common traits shared by the ruling classes of civilizations that supposedly were never in contact. It's also interesting that, despite obvious inbreeding problems, the fierceness of the world's royals to maintain genealogical purity has never waned, to the point where today virtually every European monarchy shares the same ancestors. Even more unbelievably (and creepily), according to aristocratic genealogical publisher Burke's Peerage Limited, every US president has had some French or English royal blood, including George W. Bush and Barack Obama, who happen to be eleventh cousins! Talk about keeping it in the family.

You might be asking yourself if you have enough lizard blood to join the global elite. Fair question. But it's important to note that, according to Icke, the only way for a lizard person to attain true power is to be possessed by a reptilian entity from another dimension. So unless you feel an uncontrollable evil presence taking over your brain, you're probably going to have to put those dreams of world domination on hold. Sorry.

WHAT ELSE BEGINS WITH L?

Lee Harvey Oswald

Ley Lines

Lincoln Assassination

Lindbergh Baby Kidnapping

Lockerbie Bombing

Louis Farrakhan

LSD

Luciferians

Lunar Anomalies

M
IS FOR
MOON LANDING

M is for Moon Landing, NASA's crowning achievement.

If you think it was fake, you should ask where your brain went.

But why haven't we been back? A lack of funds since the seventies?

Or did our extraterrestrial neighbors not want to share the amenities?

When composing a list of humanity's greatest achievements, traveling to the moon has to be at the very top. The unprecedented technological advancement and sheer willpower needed to make NASA's Apollo program a success still seems mind-boggling, especially for a species that was mostly riding around on horses less than a century before the July morning in 1969 when astronaut Neil Armstrong took his first small step onto the lunar surface.

Unless, of course, you're one of the thousands of moon-deniers who believe that the missions never happened. That they were simply part of an elaborate, government-funded plot to solidify America as the leader of the Space Race, a hoax filmed on secret sound stages and directed by Stanley Kubrick (yes, that Stanley Kubrick). Except that the pieces of "evidence" theorists offer as proof of the conspiracy—the supposed inability of astronauts to survive traveling through the belts of radiation surrounding the Earth, the weird shadows in the moon-landing photographs, the footage of an American flag impossibly flapping in the Moon's airless atmosphere—have all been thoroughly debunked. The Soviet Union, always more than happy to deny American accomplishments, never questioned the veracity of the Apollo missions, nor did any of the four hundred thousand people employed by the program. Also, the hundreds of moon rocks collected by astronauts, given as gifts to 135 countries, and independently analyzed in labs around the world, were found, in every case, to actually come from the, um, moon. Sorry to burst your tinfoil-covered bubble, but it's pretty clear we were there.

What's more interesting—and potentially frightening—to ponder is why we haven't been back since 1972. NASA's given a number of rational (i.e., boring) excuses for why this is the case, citing the outrageous amount of resources needed to pull off a moon shot, current budgetary restrictions, and our current political climate lacking the sense of urgency that the Cold War provided, and so on and so forth. But some people, including former NASA employee Otto Binder, tell a much more interesting story. According to Binder, many of the communications between Apollo 11 astronauts Neil Armstrong and Buzz Aldrin were allegedly censored from the public, including Aldrin noting the presence of a UFO shortly after landing on the moon's surface and Armstrong excitedly describing a fleet of parked alien spacecraft observing him from across a crater: "These 'babies' are huge, sir! Enormous! OH MY GOD! You wouldn't believe it! I'm telling you there are other spacecraft out there, lined up on the far side of the crater edge! They're on the Moon watching us!"

According to whistleblowers like former chief of NASA Communications Systems Maurice Chatelain, Armstrong and other Apollo crew members supposedly found evidence of more craft and a space station on the moon's dark side (the part that isn't visible from Earth), but weren't able to find out much because the aliens were extremely hostile and wanted the earthlings gone. While the rest of the planned Apollo missions weren't canceled—so as to not arouse public suspicion—they were apparently only "quick scoop and back again" operations because NASA was afraid of inciting our technologically superior lunar neighbors. Upon returning home, the astronauts were kindly told by the good folks at the CIA to shut the hell up about what they'd seen.

Some contemporary theorists have taken the idea of an inhabited moon to wild extremes. Proponents of the Ancient Aliens theory claim that the moon is a metallic artificial satellite, built millions of years ago by supremely intelligent beings in order to seed life on Earth with its perfectly positioned gravitational tug. Interestingly, instruments installed on the lunar surface to detect moonquakes described the moon as "ringing like a bell" during several seismic events in the 1970s. In the fall of 2019, the Indian Space Research Organisation's Chandrayaan-2 mission discovered a giant metallic mass buried near the moon's south pole before its lunar lander mysteriously crashed and something—or someone—caused it to stop functioning. Less than five months earlier, Israel's Beresheet lander was disabled in a similarly unexplained accident.

After nearly fifty years of lame excuses and possible cover-ups, it would be nice to figure out what's really going on up there. And with the US government's recent announcement of a manned mission to the moon in 2024, we may finally get some answers. I don't know about you, but I wouldn't want to be the first astronaut to take that next giant leap for mankind. Unless ending up as alien food is on your bucket list. Then you might just be in luck.

WHAT ELSE BEGINS WITH M?

Mafia

Mandela Effect

Military Industrial Complex

Mind Control

MKUltra

Monsanto

Montauk Project

N

IS FOR NAZIS IN SOUTH AMERICA

N is for the Nazis who fled in submarines across the ocean,

And landed in South America with very little commotion.

A few got caught later, but not the worst of the crew,

Like Josef "Angel of Death" Mengele (and maybe the Führer too).

The end of World War II might have marked the end of the Third Reich, but it was also a new beginning for countless Nazis who managed to flee their homeland. Thousands of the best German scientists were scooped up and pardoned by both the United States and the Soviet Union, including Wernher von Braun, an SS officer and aerospace engineer who was notoriously okay with using slave labor during the war, and who later went on to design the launch vehicle that propelled Apollo astronauts to the moon. Anything to beat the Commies . . . I guess (ick). Others, aided by Catholic clergy and networks of fascist sympathizers, took escape routes known as "ratlines" that ran through Spain or Italy and on to South America, where they settled and began new lives under assumed identities. To this day, it's common to encounter Chileans and Brazilians with German ancestry, and there are even villages in southern Argentina that resemble Bavarian mountain hamlets, where residents speak mostly German, and where cafés serve goulash, schnitzel, and steins of German beer.

That's not to say that life was totally peachy for every Nazi in the Southern Hemisphere. Agents from Israeli intelligence agency Mossad and private investigators spent decades tracking down and apprehending dozens of high-ranking German officers, assassinating them in their new homes or dragging them back to Europe or Jerusalem, where many, like major Holocaust architect Adolf Eichmann, were hung for war crimes. But they didn't catch all of them. Some of Mossad's biggest targets, including Auschwitz physician Josef "Angel of Death" Mengele and Eduard "the Butcher of Riga" Roschmann, managed to evade capture. Some researchers even insist that the most notorious Nazi—some guy you may have heard of named Adolf Hitler—was among those who disappeared into the South American countryside without a trace.

Stories that Hitler didn't actually commit suicide in the Führerbunker on April 30, 1945, have run rampant since the end of the war, when Soviet leader Joseph Stalin claimed in a press conference that his rival had staged his death, had been secreted out of Berlin, and was living in Spain or Argentina. While the statement was treated as deliberate misinformation by most Western nations, declassified FBI and CIA documents contain numerous alleged sightings of Hitler over the years, from people who supposedly saw him getting into a U-boat with his wife, Eva Braun, before crossing the Atlantic and later others who witnessed him living in various villas throughout Argentina. A former SS trooper named Phillip Citroen told American intelligence agents that Hitler had been traveling around Colombia prior to 1955, and even produced a photograph of himself and a man identified as "Adolf Schrïttelmayor," who looks very suspiciously like *the* Adolf.

Most historians are quick to dismiss the idea that Hitler escaped Berlin, citing a lack of any hard evidence, as well as the fact that dental remains discovered by Soviet soldiers in the crater where Hitler was allegedly buried were confirmed by forensic pathologists and Hitler's own dentist as belonging to the Führer. However, skull fragments that were also said to be Hitler's were re-analyzed in 2009 by an archae-ologist at the University of Connecticut, who found that they belonged to a woman in her thirties. Could Hitler have orchestrated a last-minute tooth extraction and body switch?

Whether or not you think he escaped Germany, it's kind of a moot point because it's a virtual certainty that, either way, he's been dead for a very long time. But if you happen to see a 130-year-old toothless white dude with a tiny mustache spouting fascist propaganda on your next visit to South America, be sure to alert the authorities.

WHAT ELSE BEGINS WITH N?

NASA

NBA Draft

New Chronology

New Coke

New England Patriots

Nicaragua

North American Union

NSA

IS FOR OPIOIDS

O is for Opioids, a monumental crisis,

Causing more deaths than planes, shark attacks, or ISIS.

Are the Feds or lobbyists more to blame when addiction skyrockets?

Guess it doesn't really matter when Big Pharma's lining your pockets.

Imagine you've been suffering from a debilitating long-term injury, or recovering from surgery after a traumatic accident. You've been experiencing constant physical agony so excruciating you almost feel like giving up, until your doctor swoops in with her trusty prescription pad and saves the day with a little help from Big Pharma. A pill that almost instantly erases the pain and provides a much-needed jolt of euphoria. The best part is that there aren't any major side effects (besides maybe some light constipation), and virtually no risk of dependency!

Sounds like a miracle, right?

Um, not so fast. Opioids, promoted heavily for their supposed safety and efficacy in the 1990s by American pharmaceutical giants like Purdue and Johnson & Johnson, are actually some of the most addictive and dangerous substances available for human consumption, as numerous studies have shown. Despite the threat they clearly pose to our health—and doubts about their effectiveness in treating chronic pain—these popular painkillers continue to be over-prescribed (and frequently abused), creating an epidemic of truly disturbing proportions. Drugs like hydrocodone, codeine, fentanyl, and morphine kill someone in the United States every eleven minutes. In 2017, opioids were involved in nearly two-thirds of all overdose deaths. According to the National Institute for Drug Abuse, 80 percent of heroin addicts were originally hooked on—you guessed it—opioids.

So how did things get so bad? Antidrug activists and various nonprofit organizations believe the blame lies solely with the pharmaceutical companies, who, they claim, knowingly and systematically orchestrated a massive health crisis in order to drive up profits, a practice that they say still continues. In-depth analysis of OxyContin (a brand name of the oxycodone that was first introduced by Purdue in 1996) reveals an aggressive marketing campaign that saw sales of the drug soar from $48 million to almost $1.1 billion in less than five years. The company targeted physicians who were the highest prescribers of opioids, providing them with a slew of promotional branded items and inviting them to all-expenses-paid retreats where company representatives allegedly downplayed the side effects associated with the drug. Pharmaceutical sales reps, encouraged by a wildly lucrative bonus system, allegedly began soliciting primary care physicians who weren't trained in pain management or addiction issues.

On Capitol Hill, Big Pharma lobbyists have funneled nearly $1 billion in campaign contributions to politicians to supposedly shut down any bill that might limit prescriptions and manufacturers' profit margins. Pharmaceutical advocates like the International Pain Foundation argue that any concerns about the drugs have been way overblown, and that the needs of millions of chronic pain patients outweigh any associated risks. Claiming that opioid manufacturers were initially unaware of how dangerous their pills could be, they point to new formulas being developed that make pills harder to dissolve to prevent snorting or injection. Which, according to anti-opioid crusaders, is just a sly way of remarketing an old product to further increase profits by pretending to be concerned for public welfare.

Are opioids just big business as usual, or a big-time conspiracy? Despite passionate (and well-compensated) voices on both sides of the debate, the jury's still out on this undeniably sad situation.

WHAT ELSE BEGINS WITH O?

Obama Birth Certificate

Occultism

O. J. Simpson

Operation Mockingbird

Operation Popeye

Opus Dei

Osama bin Laden

Oumuamua

P
IS FOR
PYRAMIDS

P is for the Pyramids—you've heard all the craziest stories,

That they're Atlantean power stations or ancient alien laboratories.

Why are there so many of them on every continent, of a similar variety?

Just a fluke of architecture, or remnants of a forgotten global society?

Just about everyone's familiar with the three iconic pyramids that dominate Egypt's Giza Plateau. The largest and oldest of these, the Great Pyramid, is the last surviving wonder of the ancient world and, according to most Egyptologists, was built by hundreds of thousands of workers as a tomb for the Fourth Dynasty Egyptian pharaoh Khufu around 2560 BCE. However, that narrative has been questioned recently by researchers who claim that the Giza pyramids—and similar structures around the world—are thousands of years older than mainstream archaeology suggests, serving a far different purpose than simply being monuments to dead rich guys.

Unlike many ancient Egyptian tombs and temples that are covered in hieroglyphics and illustrations, the walls of the pyramids are virtually blank. Since no bodies or other artifacts have ever been found there, Egyptologists base their entire reasoning for the age and purpose of the Great Pyramid on a tiny piece of Khufu-related graffiti and construction items that could have easily been left at the site well after its initial construction. And speaking of that construction, it's far more complex and mathematically precise than any later Egyptian architectural work, positioned at the exact geographical center of the Earth's landmass, with its multi-ton blocks fitting impeccably together and the corners of its base perfectly aligned with the four cardinal compass points. So does that mean that Egyptians defied all conventional logic about how civilizations develop and somehow got *worse* at building stuff as the centuries went on? Or do the pyramids actually predate Egypt as we understand it, to a time when most archaeologists believe that building such structures would have been impossible?

Using astronomical data, author Robert Bauval proposed in the 1970s that the layout of the Giza pyramids was in precise alignment with the three stars that form the "belt" of the constellation Orion—as they would have appeared around twelve thousand years ago. Evidence of water erosion at the base of the nearby Great Sphinx, according to geologist Robert M.

Schoch, would place the lion-shaped monument at roughly the same time period. Together, the pyramids, Sphinx, and Nile River accurately reflect Orion, fellow constellation Leo, and the Milky Way Galaxy during the astronomical Age of Leo, which began during the last Ice Age. In the 1990s, author Graham Hancock combined Bauval's and Schoch's observations to theorize that the Giza Plateau was once home to a forgotten, technologically superior progenitor civilization that was wiped out by a cataclysm around 11,800 years ago.

Hancock claims that evidence of this advanced society—similar to the one Plato described in his tales of Atlantis—exists not just at Giza, but across the world. The Mesoamerican pyramids at Teotihuacan in central Mexico are more eerily similar to Giza than any Egyptian pyramid complex, with the three most prominent ones having the same Orion-like layout as Giza's. The largest, the Pyramid of the Sun, has virtually the same size base as the Great Pyramid. Similar structures (including the por-

table, pyramidal-shaped teepees favored by many Native American tribes) exist throughout the Americas, as well as at Visoko in Bosnia and Herzegovina, where a disputed pyramid complex was discovered in 2005. There's also a pyramid buried under a mountainside in Indonesia that's still being excavated and might be as much as twenty thousand years old, and another in a remote area of China that was allegedly photographed by an American pilot at the end of World War II before the Chinese government inexplicably denied access to it, said to be exactly four times the size of the Great Pyramid and containing strange metals found nowhere else on Earth. Sphinx-like statues and depictions of reptilian or serpentine gods (maybe the Lizard People who some claim founded the Atlantean civilization?) can be observed in such seemingly incongruous locations as Peru, Cambodia, and Romania, and out-of-place artifacts like the Fuente Magna bowl—a piece of pottery discovered in Bolivia featuring markings that appear to be Sumerian cuneiform—offer further hints that the ancient world might have been a much more connected place than we've been led to believe.

Today, millions of people across the world with little else in common continue to revere pyramids as sacred objects imbued with spiritual capabilities. Take, for example, the triangular-shaped Eye of Providence, a familiar and important symbol in Christian iconography that appears hovering over an unfinished pyramid on the back of the one-dollar bill, symbolizing God's protection over the United States—or the Freemasons, or the Illuminati, depending on who you ask. Proponents of the Lost Civilization theory, as well as New Age spiritualists, suggest that pyramidal power was also a very tangible resource for the Atlanteans, who used the structures as generators to harness the Earth's natural energies for healing and other practical purposes. Like levitating massive stones, which is how ancient writers such as tenth-century Arab historian Al-Masudi claimed the pyramids were built in the first place. Sure beats lugging limestone and granite blocks around with ropes and planks for decades with thousands of your underpaid buddies, as Egyptologists suggest was the case.

Those Egyptologists, especially members of that country's highly influential Supreme Council of Antiquities (SCA), don't particularly like talk about pre–Ice Age Atlantis, energy generators, or basically anything that contradicts the Khufu/tomb narrative first put forth by English archaeologists in the nineteenth and early twentieth centuries. Probably because they like the fact that Egypt is known as the oldest and most advanced of the ancient cultures, a designation that brings in lots of tourist money (when the country's not suffering from one of its frequent civil wars). Led for decades by the dictatorial Zahi Hawass, the SCA has made a habit of publicly ridiculing anyone proposing alternative theories about the pyramids and thwarting foreign archaeological activity, allowing only two of the Great Pyramid's supposedly many interior spaces (the King's and Queen's chambers) to be explored. Hawass dismissed newly discovered passages in the 1990s and 2000s as unimportant, and discounted seismic data suggesting that mysteriously large voids exist above the King's Chamber and beneath much of the entire Giza complex.

Many archaeologists view Hawass's domineering behavior toward others in the community as stemming from a desire to promote himself and his country. But some researchers claim that the brusqueness is really a front to hide some outrageous finds that have been uncovered in secret—like a Hall of Records, which, according to twentieth-century psychic Edgar Cayce, exists under one of the Sphinx's paws and supposedly contains documents that stretch back to Atlantis and explain the "true" history of humanity. Though that might sound crazy, what's just as weird is that Hawass supposedly received a scholarship to attend the University of Pennsylvania's PhD program in Egyptology through the Association for Research and Enlightenment, an organization founded to promote Cayce's ideas. This has led some to see Hawass as nothing more than a glorified puppet, willing to cover up anything for his shady benefactors. Sure enough, when scientists using radar discovered a large cavity beneath the Sphinx, Hawass quickly labeled it a natural phenomenon and denied all access to the site. Hmm.

Regardless of whether Egyptologists are knowingly hiding information about the true origins and function of the pyramids, there are clearly some undeniable cracks in the theories they so vigorously defend. Besides the Orion correlation and weather erosion evidence, there's the gigantic and intricately designed Göbekli Tepe temple complex in Turkey that, according to even the staunchest academic historians, was built at least twelve thousand years ago when people like Hawass would claim that all humans were living in caves and throwing rocks at each other for fun; the recent dating of a thirty-one-kilometer-wide meteor crater in Greenland to exactly the same time as Hancock's theorized cataclysm; and a recent study published in the *Journal of Applied Physics* proving that the Great Pyramid is able to concentrate electromagnetic energy in its internal chambers. Add that to the Google Earth images popping up in the last few years that appear to show pyramid-like structures in Antarctica, and the time may come soon when the mainstream archaeological mafia might finally be forced to change its tune.

WHAT ELSE BEGINS WITH P?

Paranoia

Paul Is Dead

Phantom Time Hypothesis

Philadelphia Experiment

Pilgrim Society

Princess Diana

Project Blue Book

Project Paperclip

Project Pegasus

Purdue Pharma

IS FOR QANON

Q is for QAnon, born from right-wing paranoia,

As far as conspiracies go, this one definitely won't bore ya.

Liberal-worshipping Deep Staters, Hollywood pedophile rings,

Better take off that MAGA hat if you don't believe in these things.

An alleged scandal that's been referred to as Pizzagate might sound like a relatively minor, harmless controversy. Like, maybe you ordered a delicious pepperoni pie, but the delivery guy brought you one with pineapples on it instead. Ew, but not quite the end of the world, right? However, in reality, it's something much darker, part of a massive web of right-wing conspiracy theories collectively known as QAnon, where plots against United States president Donald Trump, child trafficking, Russian meddling, Satanic rituals, domestic terrorism, anti-Semitism, and violent paranoia are all par for the course. Yikes. Pineapple pizza doesn't sound so bad anymore, now does it?

This outrageous internet-based roller coaster of accusations and innuendo kicked off shortly before the US presidential election in October 2016, when a white-supremacist-linked Twitter account claimed that the New York City Police Department had uncovered email evidence of a Satanic pedophilia ring linked to prominent Democratic political figures like Hillary Clinton,

Anthony Weiner, and Clinton campaign chair John Podesta, secretly operating in places like Washington, DC's Comet Ping Pong pizzeria (hence the Pizzagate moniker). Though the Twitter account's accusations remain unsubstantiated, several pro-Trump conspiracy websites ran with the story, adding fake details that included a raid on Clinton's home and the FBI's involvement in the "case." In October 2017, a person using the account name "Q Clearance Patriot"—implying a United States Department of Energy top-secret security clearance—began making similar claims on the anonymous website 4chan, cryptically alluding to a "calm before the storm" that would end with the incarceration and/or executions of Clinton and thousands of her purported pals, like Jewish billionaires George Soros and the Rothschild banking family, and the dozens of powerful Hollywood types who are all supposedly members of the planet-controlling shadow government known as the deep state.

Who might have the guts and resources to take down such an evil, seemingly invincible cabal, to overthrow the regime and bring us into a new (Christian) utopia? According to Q, that would be none other than President Trump and his supporters, who are allegedly fighting a secret war of biblical proportions against the Satanic cultists. While there's no evidence of anything even remotely like that happening, that hasn't stopped Q from making increasingly improbable claims: that North Korean dictator Kim Jong-un is a CIA puppet; that German chancellor Angela Merkel is Adolf Hitler's granddaughter; that Trump pretended to collude with Russia in order to secretly hire Robert Mueller to spy on the Democratic Party. In response to accusations of willfully promoting untruths and having literally none of his predictions come to pass, Q has stated that "disinformation is necessary," that blatantly making up stuff helps to keep the deep state at bay . . . or something. Which, if you think about it, is kind of a brilliant way to defend yourself when you know you're utterly full of crap.

What's not so brilliant are the thousands of keyboard jockeys who take the musings of Q (or one of several alleged "Qs" said to be working together, including long-deceased John F. Kennedy Jr.) as gospel truth. These include Matthew Phillip Wright, who drove an armored truck full of weapons to the Hoover Dam in 2018, claiming he was on a mission from QAnon to demand that the Justice Department release information about the investigation into Clinton's use of a private email server; and Anthony Comello, who murdered Staten Island Mafia boss Frank Cali in 2019 because he believed Cali was a member of the deep state. QAnon-related material has been shared by conservative politicians and Fox News commentators like Sean Hannity, and has been promoted by conspiracists like Alex Jones and Jerome Corsi, celebrities like Roseanne Barr, and—perhaps most dangerously—by President Trump himself, who even invited radio host and leading QAnon activist William "Lionel" Lebron to the Oval Office for a photo op. In 2018, *Time* magazine listed Q as one of its 25 Most Influential People on the Internet, meaning, despite a more than questionable link to reality, the phenomenon is probably here to stay.

If that's the case, then it seems like there are a lot of people who would benefit from logging off the computer, taking a deep breath, going out for a walk, and enjoying a slice of pizza or two. Instead of, you know, obsessing over unlikely secret wars promoted by someone who's likely a basement-dwelling troll. Or maybe Q is right, and we're in for some truly weird end-of-days shit. Either way, hold the pineapple.

WHAT ELSE BEGINS WITH Q?

Quantum Energy Suppression

Queen Elizabeth Cannibalism

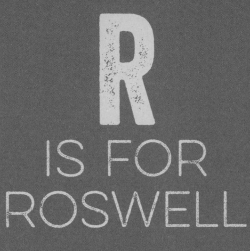

R
IS FOR
ROSWELL

R is for Roswell, a ranch where some visitors crash-landed,

The US Army cleaned it all up and then acted like they planned it.

But why the sudden bump in technology? Was it reverse-engineering?

Look at that phone in your pocket before you start jeering.

"Army Reveals It Has Flying Disc Found on Ranch in New Mexico."

If the above headline appeared today in bold print on the front (or home) page of a major newspaper, you better believe that most people—other than those predisposed to disbelieve anything involving the mainstream media—would be freaking out. Which is exactly what happened when the *Sacramento Bee* and other publications ran a report on July 8, 1947, about a saucer-shaped UFO that had crashed on a ranch outside of Roswell, New Mexico, a few weeks earlier, before being retrieved by military personnel from the nearby Roswell Army Air Field (RAAF). A day later, allegedly to squelch the public's rising curiosity and excitement about the crash, the RAAF issued a second press release stating that the debris that had been recovered was actually part of an experimental—and crudely constructed—weather balloon. Nothing to see here, folks. Move along, move along.

But despite the army's efforts to downplay the situation, the Roswell incident has, um, ballooned in pop-culture lore to become the world's most famous, most discussed, most fictionally depicted, and most investigated UFO claim. Since the 1970s—when interest in out-of-this-world phenomena began to achieve some measure of mainstream popularity—independent researchers have interviewed dozens of self-proclaimed civilian and military witnesses, performed countless hours of field work, and obtained hundreds of formerly classified documents through the Freedom of Information Act.

The consensus among most ufologists (and, according to a 1997 CNN/Time poll, most Americans) is that a spacecraft piloted by extraterrestrials did indeed plummet onto the New Mexico desert, where what was left of it—including the bodies of three-foot-tall humanoid creatures with abnormally large heads and eyes, and pieces of an impossibly strong material resembling tinfoil—was whisked away by the US government to a secret military base, such as the highly classified Area 51 in nearby Nevada. Though skeptics do make some pretty convincing counterarguments, pointing to a lack of hard evidence, the prevalence of hoaxes related to the incident (including footage of a fake alien autopsy that appeared on network television in 1995 and a 2017 *Guardian* report of Kodachrome slides depicting a dead alien that turned out to be images of a mummified Native American child), the numerous contradictions between researchers' findings (there are more than ten different locations given for where the crash supposedly occurred), and dubious deathbed confessions from elderly eyewitnesses suffering from dementia.

However, many researchers remain optimistic that proof of the crash might still be out there. While the US government has remained steadfast in its denial of anything alien-related, the US military surprisingly revealed in the 1990s that Roswell's "crashed object" had been part of a secret program called Project Mogul, and that it had been used for nuclear test surveillance. The admission inadvertently gave some credence to *The Roswell Incident* authors Charles Berlitz and William Moore, who wrote that the now-infamous flying saucer was most likely monitoring widespread nuclear weapons activity in the American Southwest before being disabled by a lightning strike. It's an idea that's echoed by many theorists and former military personnel who claim that the spike in UFO sightings during the 1940s and 1950s was a direct result of extreme extraterrestrial interest in Earth's newly acquired atomic technologies, to the point where, according to former personnel stationed at nuclear facilities around the world, UFOs would frequently appear during weapons tests and even interfere with some launches.

Whistleblower Bob Lazar, a self-described MIT-educated scientist who allegedly worked at a secret site adjacent to Area 51 in the 1980s, claims that he was tasked with reverse-engineering technology from alien spacecraft, including revolutionary components that would go on to power cell phones, other digital technology, and futuristic weapons systems. At least one of the ships supposedly had the same saucer-shaped body identical to what's described in nearly every Roswell account. After appearing in a controversial 2018 documentary about his life, Lazar's personal laboratory was raided by FBI agents, who, according to him, were looking for element 115, a substance that supposedly powers alien crafts' antimatter reactors and was considered a myth until Lazar began publicly speaking about it in the twentieth century. Shockingly, element 115 was successfully synthesized by Russian scientists in 2003, dealing a serious blow to those who viewed Lazar as little more than a crackpot.

So the hard reality is that if you're still intent on finding Roswell's smoking gun, you're probably going to have to either tamper with a nuclear missile, start a Storm Area 51 movement where people actually show up, or obtain enough advanced engineering degrees to be recruited for above-top-secret government projects (and not let your conspiracy freak flag fly during the interview), all of which, I'm sorry to say, are totally unfeasible. But so was the US government's explanation that a cute, Scotch-taped balloon fluttering harmlessly over the desert could cause the biggest UFO hoopla of all time.

WHAT ELSE BEGINS WITH R?

Race Wars

Radiation Exposure

RFID Chips

Robert Bauval

Robert M. Schoch

Robert Mueller

Rockefeller Family

Rothschild Family

IS FOR SMITHSONIAN INSTITUTION

S is for Smithsonian, the finest Institute in the country,

With a habit of losing objects that are historically funky.

Out-of-place artifacts, flying saucers, the skulls of many a cryptid,

Might change our worldview if the museum's vaults weren't restricted.

If you've ever been concerned about who really calls the shots when it comes to scientific and archaeological research, then . . . you're kind of a nerd. Just kidding—sort of—but anyways, look no further than Washington, DC. The Smithsonian Institution, founded there in 1846 with funds bequeathed by English scientist James Smithson (who, weirdly, never visited the United States), has grown to become the largest research complex in the world. With a diverse collection of approximately 154 million artifacts and specimens in its care, the "nation's attic" is an intimidatingly massive organization, one that's allegedly never been afraid to use intimidation—or manipulation, coercion, and misinformation—to advance its ideologies. And with a $1.2 billion annual budget that's mostly provided by the federal government, is that really a big surprise?

We've already discussed how the Smithsonian's staunch commitment to Darwinism and the manifest destiny of the American people in the nineteenth century allegedly led to the cover-up of an ancient civilization of giants (see page 29), but that's far from the only historical anomaly the Institution's said to have erased from public knowledge. In 1909, the *Arizona Gazette* reported that Smithsonian archaeologists S. A. Jordan and G. E. Kincaid had discovered a human-carved cave system in the Grand Canyon where they excavated a massive hoard of bizarre tablets, statues, and jewelry that appeared to be Egyptian and East Asian in origin, a find that might have changed everything we know about the settlement of the Americas.

Except that the Smithsonian later denied the report or that they'd ever employed Jordan and Kincaid. No one's been able to locate the caves since, with the possible exception of self-proclaimed Lizard Person expert John Rhodes, who warns that the entrance is guarded by a New World Order soldier wielding an M-16. Okay then. Other seemingly saner researchers have theorized that the Grand Canyon artifacts and giant bones have long been removed and stashed, along with countless other anachronistic and controversial items—ancient alien technology and extraterrestrial remains, incriminating pieces of the *Titanic*, Noah's ark, the skeletons of Bigfoot and other cryptids—in a secret underground vault beneath the National Mall, à la the final warehouse scene of *Raiders of the Lost Ark*. Which actually sounds pretty rad. Except for, you know, the whole hiding-important-stuff-from-the-public thing.

While it's fair to wonder why there haven't been more whistleblowers over the years, or why there hasn't been more of a demand for the Institution to reveal the extent of its potentially game-changing collection (of which only about 10 percent is available for public viewing), it's important to remember how much mainstream archaeologists' reputations and professional opportunities—the ability to receive grants or get university tenure—rely on maintaining the status quo. A status quo that's determined (and funded) by you-know-who. The Smithsonian's tentacles even allegedly extend to entities that are theoretically beyond its control, like the Peruvian government, which was supposedly coerced into discrediting a man who found ancient stones depicting humans interacting with dinosaur-like crea-tures, effectively shutting down any future research on them.

Fantastic beasts aside, promoting a culture of fear and suppression seems in direct opposition to John Smithson's dream of an honest establishment working openly "for the increase and diffusion of knowledge." Maybe it's time for you history and science nerds—and anyone who values transparency about where their tax dollars are going—to finally take a stand. Or convince Harrison Ford to start digging under the National Mall. Just watch out for the guys with rifles.

WHAT ELSE BEGINS WITH S?

Salem Witch Trials

Satanic Ritual Abuse

Secret Space Program

September 11

Shakespeare Authorship

Smart TV Surveillance

Stanley Kubrick

Stargates

T
IS FOR
TIME TRAVEL

T is for Time Travel, not what you've watched on the screen,

I mean stories from real people, the crazy shit that they've seen.

Secret military tests, wormholes that drop you off centuries later,

Probably best to avoid any bro with a dimensional warp generator.

Most people, at one point or another, have imagined what it would be like to visit time periods other than their own. Maybe to get definitive answers about disputed historical events like the construction of Stonehenge, the fall of Rome, or the Knicks actually being relevant. Or, to marvel at the inconceivable advancements of future civilizations (barring any apocalypses, of course). While time travel features prominently in countless works of science fiction and folklore, a few fortunate—or profoundly unlucky—souls have allegedly experienced the phenomenon firsthand, with a handful returning to discuss their far-out journeys.

In the 1950s, rumors began to circulate through the UFO community about a secret experiment that had been conducted at the Philadelphia Navy Shipyard in the fall of 1943. According to researcher Morris K. Jessup and other theorists, military scientists used an unknown electromagnetic technology to render the destroyer escort USS *Eldridge* totally invisible; then teleported the warship to either New York or Virginia; then sent it to another dimension; and then ten seconds backward in time. Many of the ship's crew apparently died or suffered horrific injuries when the ship reappeared, including some whose bodies physically fused to the ship's bulkhead or rematerialized with their insides on the outside.

Not wanting to turn into a real-life version of the Operation game, a young sailor named Al Bielek allegedly jumped overboard before the Eldridge went totally batty and somehow woke up in a hospital covered in radiation burns—in the year 2137! Six weeks later, he was mysteriously transported to 2749, where people lived peacefully in domed, floating cities controlled by benevolent socialist computers that provided everything they needed. After two years of living the futuristic good life and learning about the previous seven hundred years of human history, Bielek returned to 2137 to scoop up his brother Duncan (who'd also jumped ship) before teleporting back to the twentieth century. He was then allegedly recruited by the US government and/or military to work on several top-secret projects at underground facilities on Long Island. Collectively known as the Montauk Project, these experiments allegedly led to breakthroughs in exotic fields like mind control, psychological warfare, and bioengineering (Montauk Monster, anyone?). Bielek claimed that the scientists there had learned how to master the space-time continuum and used this technology to send him to Mars, a research station in 100,000 BCE, and various planets in the year 6037 to obtain canisters filled with light and dark Energy. (Because hey, why not?)

Though Bielek's wild story has been debunked by both mainstream killjoys and open-minded indie researchers—and disproven by his own inaccurate predictions of twenty-first-century events—there are plenty of other reports of alleged time travel incidents. Several films from the 1920s and 1930s, including Charlie Chaplin's *The Circus,* appear to show potential millennial time travelers wielding smartphones. Rudolph Fentz, the victim of a 1950s Manhattan taxi accident, was found wearing 1800s clothing and carrying a bill for a carriage washing and matched the NYPD's description of someone who disappeared in 1876—though it's possible that one was actually an embellishment of a short story by sci-fi author Jack Finney. Then there's the hard-to-explain case of Andrew Carlssin, a Wall Street wunderkind who apparently came out of nowhere in 2003 and turned an initial stock market investment of $800 into $350 million in just two weeks. Before disappearing again, he was questioned by authorities about his impossible "luck," and claimed that he was from two hundred years in the future and had gone back in time to make a little extra cash, a move that would have made Marty McFly proud. That same year, a mass spam email found its way to thousands of inboxes, from a self-proclaimed time traveler looking for a lost "dimensional warp generator." Perhaps Carlssin wasn't as slick as he seemed.

Perhaps it's time to stop debating whether time travel is real or not—especially forward time travel, which quantum physics has pretty much shown to be technically viable—and figure out how to teleport directly to the 2749 government-free robot utopia that Bielek described. Or maybe head back a few years to make some "lucky" tech investments. Either way, as the indie rock band The Replacements famously opined, "Anywhere's better than here."

WHAT ELSE BEGINS WITH T?

Technology Suppression

Ted Cruz

Tesla Coil

Thrive (film)

Tom DeLonge

Trump-Russia Collusion

Tupac Shakur

Turin Shroud

U
IS FOR
UNITED NATIONS

U is for United Nations, an organization built for peace,

Or a cleverly concealed death machine born to make this world cease?!

Globalist schemers, population purgers, manipulators of morale,

Best to steer clear of these folks unless you're the Antichrist's pal.

For a planet as fractured and contentious as the one most of us reside upon, the United Nations (UN) sounds like a refreshingly noble concept: an international forum where all countries are granted an equal say, where leading diplomats and politicians can peacefully and neutrally air out their grievances, while keeping a stern eye on any human rights violations or other injustices that might arise. Not surprisingly, that concept hasn't really taken hold in a little place called the real world. Since its formation in the aftermath of World War II, the UN has suffered from constant squabbling between members with vastly different ideologies, a lack of sufficient funding, and not being taken seriously by virtually anyone it tries to sanction.

Beyond the public shitshow, the UN, as a global body, has predictably been linked to an impressive number of conspiracies. The organization has been accused of being a vehicle for the usual suspects—Illuminati, New World Order, Freemasons, the Catholic Church, Jewish bankers, Communists, Lizard People—who all allegedly share similar globalist agendas and want to profit from erasing national borders. One of the main ways the UN's schemers plan on achieving a one-world state, according to right-wing theorists, is by being nice to the planet, specifically the promotion of climate change propaganda like Agenda 21, a set of guidelines for environmental action and social justice established by the UN in 1992. The initiative has inexplicably been described by former Fox News host Glenn Beck as an attempt by Nazi communist internationalist homosexuals to "put their fangs into our communities and suck all the blood out of it," an idea that's been echoed by various religious types and the Republican National Committee, which condemned Agenda 21 as a "comprehensive plan of extreme environmentalism, social engineering, and global political control" that will supposedly replace Christianity with a pagan Earth-worshipping cult. Alrighty then.

Taking things a step further, some evangelical groups argue that malicious hippie tree huggers are the least of our worries, that our planet's diplomats are actually beholden to forces which are literally out of this world. They warn that the UN is under the direct control of Satan and his pal the Antichrist, as described in the Book of Revelation. The organization apparently is the physical embodiment of the Harlot "Sitting atop the Nations, Multitudes, Languages, and Tongues" with its globe-depicting flag representing the "image of a wild beast" that will soon act to destroy all countries and religions.

But it gets even better. Other alleged insiders have described the UN as being manipulated by interplanetary entities with the capabilities to make Revelation look like a walk in the park. According to self-proclaimed US military black-ops employee Corey Goode, there are currently five secret space programs that have been operating for decades, using *Star Trek*–level extraterrestrial technology to run amok throughout the solar system and beyond. One of these, the Global Galactic League of Nations (GGLN), founded in part by Ronald Reagan in the 1980s as a direct offshoot of the UN, supposedly works to protect Earth from alien threats. Which sounds cool, except that Goode claims that the GGLN has actually been infiltrated and manipulated by the much more powerful Interplanetary Corporate Conglomerate, a group of corporate overlords, technocrats, and über-evil Reptilians who apparently want nothing more than to enslave the minds and bodies of every sentient being in the galaxy. Oops. Looks like global bureaucracy is just as ineffective in space as it is on Earth. Of all of Goode's disclosures, that one's probably the least surprising.

WHAT ELSE BEGINS WITH U?

UFOs

Underwater Bases

US Government

USS *Cyclops*

USS *Eldridge*

USS *Nimitz*

IS FOR
VACCINES

V is for Vaccines, the more that get them the merrier,

Though some say your doctor might be up to something scarier.

Injecting autism for profit, on the whim of some evil corporate fella?

Have fun explaining that crap when your kid gives you rubella.

Vaccines are generally viewed as one of the greatest success stories in the field of public health. Since 1798, when English physician Edward Jenner demonstrated that an injectable preparation of cowpox could prevent smallpox infections, doctors have spared millions of patients from potentially life-threatening viruses like smallpox, diphtheria, polio, and hepatitis by exposing them to weakened forms of disease-causing microorganisms in order to stimulate their bodies' immune systems. Today, getting vaccinated is seen as a rite of passage for more than 90 percent of American infants and toddlers, with most public schools requiring a measles, mumps, and rubella (MMR) shot as a nonnegotiable condition of enrollment.

Despite their proven efficacy at preventing (and in some cases eradicating) viral outbreaks, vaccines have come under greater scrutiny than ever before. Because, apparently, some people can't have nice things. Or maybe what we've been led to believe is a nice thing isn't what it's cracked up to be. You'd have to ask one of the thousands of anti-vaccine advocates, who, despite widespread ridicule from the medical community and a constant barrage of hilariously savage memes on social media, continue to vigorously promote their agenda. Basically, anti-vaxxers feel that vaccine requirements infringe on their personal and religious liberties; that most doctors are immoral, uneducated (huh?), and, along with profit-hungry pharmaceutical manufacturers, the mainstream media, and the US government, knowingly spread misinformation about vaccines' chemical contents and deliberately fail to disclose the potential for adverse vaccine reactions like autism; and that homeopathic remedies are equally effective at treating illnesses.

It's true that no vaccination—or any other medical procedure—is ever 100 percent safe, and that many vaccines do contain questionable substances like aluminum and mercury, which have been reduced in recent years. Mishaps like the 1955 Cutter incident, in which 120,000 doses of Salk's polio vaccine were accidentally infused with a live polio virus, have caused minor health crises and even a handful of deaths. And for those of the anti-establishment ilk, it might seem a little fishy that Donald Trump, a frequent anti-vaccination tweeter in the mid-2010s, suddenly and inexplicably changed his stance after becoming president, imploring citizens to "get their shots" after a measles outbreak in early 2019. But despite the occasional instance of bad publicity, there's never been any legitimate study that definitively links vaccines to increased incidents of autism. Vaccines are some of the most highly monitored and tested substances in history, with the FDA committed to working with companies to develop safer manufacturing protocols and requiring that vaccines undergo three phases of clinical trials with human subjects before they can be licensed for use in the general public. Which, according to anti-vaxxers, is exactly what the Big Bad Government and Big Pharma want you to believe.

Ultimately, for parents trying to figure out whether to vaccinate their child, it's a matter of who to trust. Do you side with leading anti-vaccine activists like former Playmate Jenny McCarthy, who rose to fame hosting MTV's *Singled Out* for three years? Or do you listen to your doctor, who went to medical school for twice as long and took an oath to hold your health in the highest regard? Given the disturbing spike in preventable disease outbreaks in the last few years (including the first confirmed death from measles in twelve years in 2015 and a 2019 mumps outbreak at Philadelphia's Temple University that infected more than one hundred people), that choice apparently isn't as easy as it seems.

WHAT ELSE BEGINS WITH V?

Vatican Library

Vladimir Putin

Vril Society

W

IS FOR
WALT DISNEY

W is for Walt, or Mister Disney to most people,

Who loved life so much he secretly planned for a sequel.

Rumor is he's buried under his theme park, cryogenically dozin',

Is it just a blockbuster of a hoax, or the original *Frozen*?

Any entrepreneur who can parlay a talking rodent into a multinational mass media and entertainment conglomerate is clearly someone capable of thinking outside the box. One of the twentieth century's greatest innovators, film producers, and all-around visionaries, Walter Elias "Walt" Disney always had a feel for the next big thing, from pioneering ambitious animation techniques that would shape the medium into a giant cultural force, to totally redefining and vastly expanding the idea of what an amusement park could be.

Not surprisingly, the Man Behind the Mouse was also a noted futurist. Disney collaborated with NASA's Wernher von Braun (see page 60) on several space exploration films in the 1950s and developed a Space Age–themed area of Disneyland called Tomorrowland in order for guests to "participate in adventures that are a living blueprint of our future." In 1982, the Disney Company massively expanded on the concept when it opened the EPCOT (Experimental Prototype Community of Tomorrow) theme park at the Walt Disney World Resort.

But many believe Disney's most ambitious futuristic achievement occurred immediately after his death from lung cancer in 1966. Namely, that his body was cryogenically frozen by scientists and buried deep beneath Disneyland's Pirates of the Caribbean ride, where he'll remain in suspended animation until medical science has advanced enough to reanimate him. Nice. No one's really sure where or when the fantastically frigid story took off, but since the late 1960s, Disney's inner circle has categorically denied that ole Walt's been stashed away on ice beneath the Southern California soil. Disney's daughter Diane wrote in her autobiography that her father probably hadn't even heard of the spanking-new science of cryonics (which seems kind of odd considering her father's obsession with advanced technologies). One Disney executive blamed the rumor on a group of mischievous animators who wanted to get one last laugh at the expense of their newly deceased boss. That's done little to detract proponents of the theory, who point to the secretive nature of Disney's funeral and burial—both were closed off to the public—and his preoccupation with his own death, as noted in several posthumous biographies. And honestly, does it really seem too farfetched to think that someone responsible for something as trippy as *Fantasia* might attempt an equally wacky act of self-preservation?

The image of a slumbering cryo-Walt began to slide off the pop-culture radar in the 2000s, but the idea has been recently, um, brought back to life on the internet after the arrival of another ice-filled Disney property. The idea is that the Disney Company created the 2013 animated film *Frozen* so that whenever anyone googles "Walt Disney Frozen," articles related to the movie appear instead of ruminations on the whereabouts of Walt's corpse. While the effectiveness of a strategy like that is suspect at best (it's really easy to find articles about any of this stuff), it does make sense from a marketing perspective. I mean, wouldn't you rather spend your time on the Pirates of the Caribbean ride pretending to be Jack Sparrow than thinking about the undecomposed body of an old white dude that might be lying directly under your feet?

Cryogenics has advanced greatly in the last fifty years or so, with companies charging up to $200,000 to put clients in a deep-freeze state, meaning that Disney's alleged quest for immortality might become a reality. But for the hundreds of people whose bodies are already waiting in cryonic sleep, the science to revive them is still far, far away from viability. So, if you really want to know what happened to Walt Disney, you're probably going to have to cough up a few bucks and literally chill out for a few centuries to find out.

WHAT ELSE BEGINS WITH W?

War Against Islam

War on Christmas

War on Drugs

Warren Commission

Watergate

Wernher von Braun

World Health Organization

X

IS FOR PLANET X

X is the ninth planet that some say orbits our sun,

Every 3,600 years, it gets close to Earth for some fun.

And by fun, I mean: Disaster!

Our world completely spun off its axis!

Sure, apocalypses suck, but at least you won't have to do taxes.

Where do we come from?

It's one of humanity's most important—and perplexing—questions, one that's confounded scientists and philosophers since at least the beginning of written history, and probably way before that. But for the ancient Sumerians and Babylonians, as translated by ancient astronaut theorist Zecharia Sitchin, the answer was easy: Nibiru. According to Sitchin's interpretations of various Mesopotamian religious texts, that was the name of a massive planet with an irregular orbit that passes close to Earth every 3,600 years, allowing its technologically advanced inhabitants to interact with our planet. Those would be the Annunaki, giant man-fish-bird-looking creatures who supposedly combined their own DNA with that of *homo erectus* five hundred thousand years ago to create modern humans, who they promptly enslaved and forced to mine gold. Fortunately for us, they realized what huge jerks they were being after the Antarctic glaciers melted (causing the biblical Great Flood) and they decided to teach humans useful stuff like agriculture to help them rebuild civilization. According to Sitchin, they then took off in their spaceships and went back to their home world, only to return the next time Nibiru approaches Earth. Though far less entertaining than sagas about god-like, gold-crazed aliens, the theories of early twentieth-century astronomer Percival Lowell—namely, that the irregularities in the orbits of gas giants like Neptune and Uranus might be caused by a large unseen world he dubbed Planet X—brought those ancient myths into the realm of scientific possibility.

While most mainstream astronomers scoff at the existence of such a world in our solar system (even as a few continue to speculate that an undiscovered "super-Earth" could be altering the orbits of several dwarf planets beyond Neptune), that hasn't stopped internet doomsday enthusiasts from predicting cataclysmic events stemming from an alleged interplanetary encounter with X/Nibiru. Chief among these folks is Nancy Lieder, founder of the website ZetaTalk, who believes that extraterrestrials called Zetans implanted a communications device in her brain when she was a child and use it to contact her. In the 1990s, she claimed the Zetans told her that the Hale-Bopp comet was a hoax created by NASA and others in power to distract people from the arrival of Planet X on May 27, 2003, which would apparently force Earth's rotation to cease, causing unprecedented natural disasters and the end of humanity.

When nothing happened, similar-minded theorists proposed later dates for the collision, many choosing December 21, 2012, to align with the end of a cycle in the Mayan Long Count calendar. Nope, sorry. Not to be deterred, Christian numerologist David Meade claimed to have used secret numerological passages in the Bible to arrive at an apocalypse date of October 5, 2017, when Planet X would eclipse the sun, sparking a worldwide nuclear war, unprecedented earthquakes, a magnetic pole shift, the destruction of half of the United States, and Barack Obama's election to a third presidential term. Well, we all know how that worked out.

Though hiding the imminent arrival of a potentially life-threatening planetary body from the public wouldn't be the worst strategy for NASA, as far as preventing the immediate collapse of society, it would probably be impossible to accomplish. As several scientists have pointed out, even backyard astronomers would be able to detect Planet X long before it reaches Earth. And even if Sitchin's translations are accurate (which other Sumerian scholars loudly deny), Nibiru's next brush with Earth won't be until the year 2900 or thereabouts. So, unless you hope to one day use artificial intelligence to upload your brain and spend the next few centuries cruising around as an immortal cyborg dreading the alleged return of alien slave-masters, there's probably nothing to worry about.

WHAT ELSE BEGINS WITH X?
X-Files
X-rays

IS FOR YETI

Y is for Yeti, who makes no apology,

The undisputed king of cryptozoology.

His bellow and stench wither the hearts of the brave

And might make you think twice before you visit a cave.

Yeti. Sasquatch. The Abominable Snowman. Bigfoot. Throughout the world, in the oral and written traditions of far-flung cultures, legends exist of six- to nine-foot-tall, bipedal, ape-like creatures lurking in dense forests and remote mountainous areas. For the last hundred years or so, these stories have stepped out of the realm of obscure folklore and left an indelible mark on popular culture, with yetis being depicted in countless horror movies, songs, video games, works of literature, and unintentionally terrifying Claymation Christmas TV specials.

But for the dozens of eyewitnesses who claim to have caught a glimpse of one of the impressively hairy (and supposedly putrid-smelling) critters each year, the myths quickly—and often shockingly—dissolve into something far more real. Occurring mostly in the Himalayas and the Pacific Northwest, Yeti sightings have inspired numerous scientists and explorers, including famed Everest conqueror Sir Edmund Hillary and his trusty Sherpa Tenzing Norgay, to devote significant resources toward finding definitive proof of the elusive cryptid. Today,

nongovernmental organizations, such as the Sasquatch Genome Project, spend countless hours analyzing the thousands of (mostly questionable) photographed and cast footprints, hair samples, and films/videos that continue to be collected by dedicated researchers.

Though some Asian nations like Nepal legally consider the yeti to be a real animal (and even require permits for yeti-hunting expeditions), and despite the opinions of well-regarded figures like primatologist Jane Goodall, most of the Western world remains skeptical, chalking up sightings to bears or other common mammals. It's a classic example of "Show me the money!" (or, in this case, "Show me the giant smelly gorilla-man corpse!").

Some researchers believe that indisputable evidence has existed at various times but has either been destroyed or covered up. There's a compelling glass-plate photograph taken in 1894 in the wilds of western Canada by fur trappers that seems to depict a captured or murdered yeti lying on the snow with its hairy hands and body clearly visible. According to writing found on the reverse side, the photo was one of several depicting the creature. But the others were apparently confiscated by a member of the Hudson's Bay Company—a powerful organization that owned 15 percent of the land mass of North America at the time—who didn't want to scare away other trappers from doing business in the area.

In 1959, nine people died of mysterious circumstances near the Dyatlov Pass in the northern Ural Mountains in the then Soviet Union. Members of the search party who found the impossibly mangled bodies claimed that large footprints they saw near the site (and not included in any reports), as well as suppressed recordings of unique howling sounds, were indications of a military cover-up. Not to be outdone by the Commies, the FBI opened up its own yeti investigation in 1976, when Oregonian Peter Byrne of the Bigfoot Information Center and Exhibition sent the Bureau hair and skin fragments for analysis. According to the now-declassified file, the FBI determined that the hairs belonged to a deer and returned them to Byrne. Far from being dissuaded, yeti believers feel that the fact that a predominantly crime-fighting organization would take Byrne's samples seriously is clear proof that *something* is out there. Also, Byrne claims that the FBI never returned the hairs to him, even though the report states that they had. Which totally seems like something the FBI would do.

If you're dead-set on being the first person to prove the yeti's existence, there are dozens of companies offering intimate tours of the regions where the creatures are alleged to inhabit. But if you do find some compelling evidence, you might want to hold onto it until the sticklers in charge of Big Science and various government agencies are more amenable to accepting things that are a little out of the ordinary. So basically, like, forever.

WHAT ELSE BEGINS WITH Y?
Yellowcake Uranium

Z
IS FOR
ZEITGEIST

Z is for Zeitgeist, the spirit of our society,

We're more connected than ever, so what's with the anxiety?

Fake news, government lies, it's enough to make anyone feel sordid,

I'd suggest some fresh air, unless you're scared of being recorded . . .

According to the Oxford English Dictionary (and some nineteenth-century German philosopher bros), *Zeitgeist* is a term that refers to the "defining spirit or mood of a particular period of history as shown by the ideas and beliefs of the time." For the 1960s, it was a sense of exhilarating transformation fueled by free love, progressive sociopolitical movements, and the Space Race. The arrival of cell phones, personal computers, cable news, and other mass-produced digital technology turned the individualistic 1980s into what the *Los Angeles Times* called an "age of Culture Lite, a consumer-driven wasteland," countering the counterculture with Reaganomics and shopping mall arcades (and don't forget *Top Gun*!).

What about now? How do we define our own uniquely turbulent era with a brief phrase or a couple of snazzy buzzwords? That's probably impossible, but there are some decent options out there: interconnectivity, information/misinformation overload, a heightened mistrust of authority, unauthorized surveil- lance, powerlessness in the face of climate change, environmental catastrophes, fascism, etc., and—perhaps slightly less depressingly— the arrival of meme culture. All of these have contributed greatly to another phenomenon of our times: the unprecedented rise of conspiracy theories. No longer solely ridiculed as the insane ramblings of tinfoil-hat-wearing forty-year-olds in their parents' basements, conspiracies are discussed openly by the international media and endorsed by celebrities, athletes, and, ahem, certain world leaders. Today, self-proclaimed "red-pillers"—those who, like Keanu Reeves in *The Matrix*, choose to cast away the safety net of conventional, mainstream thinking and wade into the murky waters of the conspiracy landscape and its countless YouTube videos, subreddits, and paranoia-inducing blog rants—come in all shapes and sizes. Some even live aboveground!

So why have conspiracies become so popular? The internet certainly provides conspiracists with a far-reaching and often professional-seeming platform (one that's slightly more palatable than the age-old strategy of screaming and throwing homemade pamphlets at randos in the street); it's hard to imagine events like the so-called 2012 Mayan Apocalypse or theories about the Flat Earth even registering on the pop-culture radar without people constantly tweeting and posting about them. But studies show that the receptiveness to conspiracies goes beyond their in-your-face presence on social media. Alienation also plays a major part. Those who have lost a job, an election, or influence in their community frequently look for anonymous forces—usually ones outside of their political party and wealth demographic—to blame, like Satanic city slicker Libtards or alien-loving NASA eggheads who are the talk of countless message boards.

It's hard to think of a time in recent history when the societal divide has been so cavernous, when populism has been as frustratingly popular or as encouraged by those in power. One aspect of our selfie-obsessed era that does bridge the culture gap is the desire for uniqueness, to stand out in a crowd (or on Instagram). Yet this too fuels the conspiracy machine. When your hits, likes, and page views continue to pile up, when you can just scream "fake news!" at anyone who opposes you, who cares about the facts or the evidence? For many, it's much better than the alternative: admitting that maybe, just maybe, they're probably a bit nuts, and more than a little lonely.

Now more than ever before, people are going to believe what they want to believe, regardless of how irrational or illogical it may seem to others. In some ways, it makes sense. Undoubtedly, it's a hell of a lot more exhilarating to inhabit a place where you can blame your problems on the reptilian elite or mind-control drugs in your tap water, rather than face the reality of a mundane world where everything's as it seems, and where politicians can inflict real damage without the backing of demon-worshipping secret societies. In a weird way, it's almost more comforting to imagine a sinister cabal behind JFK's murder than one random disgruntled gunman. It's also dangerous. Just ask the hundreds of children who contracted measles in the last few years because their parents accepted a fantasy narrative over common sense.

But go ahead and take a little dive down the rabbit hole every once in a while. It can be fun. Just don't dig so deep that you get stuck in an inescapable, tinfoil-covered pit of paranoia and self-delusion. Because, in all likelihood, there won't be any little green men to beam you back to safety. If there are, tell them to come pick me up next.

WHAT ELSE BEGINS WITH Z?

Zahi Hawass

Zecharia Sitchin

Zionism

Zodiac Killer

FURTHER READING

Alien World Order: The Reptilian Plan to Divide and Conquer the Human Race by Len Kasten (Bear & Company, 2017)

America Before: The Key to Earth's Lost Civilization by Graham Hancock (St. Martin's Press, 2019)

The Ancient Giants Who Ruled America: The Missing Skeletons and the Great Smithsonian Cover-Up by Richard J. Dewhurst (Bear & Company, 2013)

The Book of Earths: Hollow Earth, Ancient Maps, Atlantis, and Other Theories by Edna Kenton (Forgotten Books, 2008)

Chemtrails, HAARP, and the Full Spectrum Dominance of Planet Earth by Elana Freeland (Feral House, 2014)

Conspiracies Declassified: The Skeptoid Guide to the Truth Behind the Theories by Brian Dunning (Adams Media, 2018)

The Day After Roswell by Philip J. Corso and William J. Birnes (Atria Books, 1999)

The Devil's Chessboard: Allen Dulles, the CIA, and the Rise of America's Secret Government by David Talbot (Harper Perennial, 2016)

Fingerprints of the Gods by Graham Hancock (Three Rivers Press, 1996)

Fluoride: Drinking Ourselves to Death by Barry Groves (Newleaf, 2002)

Grey Wolf: The Escape of Adolf Hitler by Simon Dunstan and Gerrard Williams (Sterling, 2011)

Hoax: A History of Deception: 5,000 Years of Fakes, Forgeries, and Fallacies by Ian Tattersall and Peter Névraumont (Black Dog & Leventhal, 2018)

The Illuminati: The Secret Society That Hijacked the World by Jim Marrs (Visible Ink Press, 2017)

Into the Bermuda Triangle: Pursuing the Truth Behind the World's Greatest Mystery by Gian J. Quasar (International Marine/Ragged Mountain Press, 2005)

J. Edgar Hoover: The Man and the Secrets by Curt Gentry (W. W. Norton & Company, 2001)

Kennedy's Last Stand: Eisenhower, UFOs, MJ-12 & JFK's Assassination by Michael E. Salla (Exopolitics Institute, 2013)

Monsters Among Us: An Exploration of Otherworldly Bigfoots, Wolfmen, Portals, Phantoms, and Odd Phenomena by Linda S. Godfrey (TarcherPerigee, 2016)

The Montauk Project: Experiments in Time by Peter Moon and Preston B. Nichols (Sky Books, 1992)

Planet X, the Sign of the Son of Man, and the End of the Age by Doug Elwell (Defender, 2010)

The Suppressed History of America: The Murder of Meriwether Lewis and the Mysterious Discoveries of the Lewis and Clark Expedition by Paul Schrag and Xaviant Haze (Bear & Company, 2011)

Who Really Killed Kennedy? by Jerome R. Corsi (WND Books, 2013)

ACKNOWLEDGMENTS

Infinite thanks, as always, to the people who create the environment that allows me to do my work, including my incredible agent, Rica Allanic; my indispensably insightful editors, Emma Brodie and Nate Lanman; and the whole team at Morrow Gift. Gratitude forever to illustrator Keni Thomas and your ability to make all these crazy ideas look far cooler than I could have imagined. And a special thanks to anyone willing to keep an open mind in these incomparably weird times.

HarperCollins books may be purchased for educational,
business, or sales promotional use. For information, please
email the Special Markets Department at
SPsales@harpercollins.com.

FIRST EDITION

Designed by Bonni Leon-Berman

Library of Congress Cataloging-in-Publication Data has been applied for.

ISBN 978-0-06-299429-5

20 21 22 23 24   IM   10 9 8 7 6 5 4 3 2 1